Romano-British Curse Tablets

The Religious and Spiritual Romanization of Ancient Britain

Colleen M. Bradley

TABLE OF CONTENTS

LIST OF TABLES

LIST OF FIGURES

ACKNOWLEDGMENTS

This book is an adaptation of my Master of Arts in History thesis from San Francisco State University, and it owes much to the continued support and guidance of my thesis committee, Richard Hoffman, Laura Lisy-Wagner, and Jarbel Rodriguez. I would like to thank the following people for their help in editing some of the early sections of this book, acquiring sources for this book, and general advice: Dan Brooker, Nathan Daniels, Megan Garedakis, Frankie Griffen, Astrid Smith, Catie Steinman, and Keith Terry. A big thank you to Rachael Kerrigan, Elena Martinez, and Eugene Smelyansky for going above and beyond in unearthing some hard to find sources. I would like to thank my parents, Marilyn and Bill Wilson, for fostering my love of learning. Most of all, I would like to thank Mark Bradley for translating Celtic for me, helping me see different points of view in Romano-Celtic relations, and for encouraging me in everything I do.

Introduction

They were once ruled by kings, but are now divided under chieftains into factions and parties. Our greatest advantage in coping with tribes so powerful is that they do not act in concert. Seldom is it that two or three states meet together to ward off a common danger. Thus, while they fight singly, all are conquered.[1]

For 366 years Rome controlled a large portion of the island of Britain.[2] The political and military means that Rome employed to rule the province have been well documented by authors from Cornelius Tacitus to Martin Henig. Yet the social and religious histories of Roman Britain have rarely been investigated. While the study of history is becoming more focused on social aspects of the past, the study of Romano-British history is almost completely confined to the world of the most wealthy and powerful inhabitants of Roman Britain. Focusing on the curse tablets found in Britain, this work examines the lives of average Romano-Britons, which have not been adequately explored and are much more difficult to uncover than military, political, or economic history.

Even at the height of the Roman presence in Britain, most of the residents of the province were natives. While it is well established that the native Britons experienced great political, social, and economic changes, changes in daily life and spiritual beliefs were not well recorded.[3] Information on the religion, rituals, and beliefs of the Romano-Britons is severely lacking. Cataloging what was Celtic and what was Roman in Roman Britain is pointless; anything created on the shores of this most isolated province was neither truly Celtic nor Roman. It was Romano-British. These two worlds blended into one, creating a culture neither superior nor inferior to it parents cultures, something wholly exceptional, even amongst the far flung Roman provinces.

There are two serious problems with the sources on pre-Roman and Roman

---

[1] Cornelius Tacitus, *The Life of Cnæus Julius Agricola* Translated by Alfred John Church and William Jackson Brodribb (New York: Random House, 1942), 12.

[2] There is a debate as to when the Romans really "left" Britain, although 410 is the traditional date, for more see Michael E. Jones, *The End of Roman Britain* (Ithaca: Cornell University Press, 1996), 246-252.

[3] Cornelius Tacitus, *The Annals* Volume 5 Translated by John Jackson (Cambridge, MA: Harvard University Press, 1981), books 12.31-12.39; Tacitus, *Agricola* 5- 40 gives a general outline of the first generation after the conquest; Dio Cassius, *Roman History* Translated by Earnest Cary (Cambridge, MA: Harvard University Press, 1982): 60.19-23, 62.1-12.

Britain: their scarcity and their bias. Many literary sources that are most commonly invoked, such as Caesar, Tacitus, and Dio, are grossly inaccurate.[4] Sometimes these errors are intentional. Caesar needed justification to conquer the Celts, and invariably wrote some lies about the Celts, in order to make the Celtic culture appear repugnant to Romans, an affront to Roman sensibilities.[5] Tacitus, on the other hand, wished to praise his own father-in-law, who helped establish Roman rule in Britain, as well as condemning Roman luxury by praising the Briton's simplicity.[6]

Many other authors gave an inaccurate view of life on the British Isles not because of malice, but to entertain their audiences. The reversal of Classical norms was the most efficient way to do this.[7] Although Posidonius claimed that the Britons were so backwards that they did not use olive oil, archeological evidence has proved that olive oil was being traded to Britain.[8] Yet while perpetuating the fictitious and the fantastic, many authors managed to omit insightful information that was known by many Romans who had visited Britain. The stone henges and massive artificial mounds that dotted the British landscape were never mentioned in any work of literature. Yet the Romans knew about these features, and the mound of Avebury was even used by Roman road-builders to survey terrain.[9]

Epigraphic evidence from Roman Britain is scarce, making it not much superior to the available literary sources. The only places with prolific epigraphic data are London and the other *coloniae*.[10] The lack of written evidence from Britain is understandable; it was one of the remotest provinces and had few monuments, and thus, few epigraphic sources. There are approximately 2500

---

[4] G. B. Townend, "Some Rhetorical Battle-Pictures in Dio," *Hermes* 92, no. 4 (1964): 467, and J. P. V. D. Balsdon, "The Veracity of Caesar," *Greece & Rome*, Second Series. 4, no. 1 (1957): 19.

[5] Caesar's politically motivated distortions do not make his writings invalid, but they do make it dangerous to use his works as the basis of any statement. His distortion of the Germans was elaborated in J. P. V. D. Balsdon, "The Veracity of Caesar," 22ff. Another example is Caesar's description of the aftermath of the Battle of Pharsalus, as noted in Andreola Rossi, "The Camp of Pompey: Strategy of Representation in Caesar's Bellum Ciuile," *The Classical Journal* 95, No. 3 (2000): 240-241.

6 Tacitus, *Agricola*, 21.

7 P. C. N. Stewart, "Inventing Britain: The Roman Creation and Adaptation of an Image," *Britannia* 26 (1995): 6.

8 Joan P. Alcock, *Food in Roman Britain* (Stroud: Tempus, 2001), 77.

[9] Aubrey Burl, *Prehistoric Avebury*, 2nd ed. (New Haven: Yale University Press, 2002), 172.

[10] Graham Webster, *The British Celts and Their Gods Under Rome* (London: B. T. Batsford Ltd., 1986), 80.

inscriptions that have been discovered in Roman Britain, whereas the city of Rome has 20,000 funerary inscriptions.[11] Britain's isolation from the rest of the Empire meant that few Romans immigrated to the island beyond those who were posted there with the army. Few local records survived, as they were generally on stylus tablets, which were wax on wood, or thin slices of wood.[12]

Archeological evidence is needed to fill in the many gaps in the literary and epigraphic evidence. However, there are problems with the archeological evidence. Archeological finds are often put in small museums that do not have the funds to preserve or publish findings, so some of what has been dug up is still unknown to the academic community.[13] Many archeological finds have been unearthed, yet it is unclear as to what the objects were and what they meant to the people who created and owned them. Many items are labeled votive offerings simply because their true purpose has not yet been ascertained. Even the best understood objects do not mean to us what they meant to the Romano-Britons. British artifacts contained symbols and layers of meaning that are incomprehensible to those from outside their unique cultural context.

An overlooked source of information about Roman Britain is the numerous curse tablets that have been found in the province. The curse tablets are rarely studied, although they could be incredibly informative, especially given the lack of other epigraphic sources. Several scholars, such as Graham Webster, Lindsay Allason-Jones, and Marilynne Raybould have suggested utilizing the information in curse tablets in order to better understand the Romano-British people, yet few have taken the time to analyze the tablets.[14] With careful examination, these tablets can help illuminate the religious and spiritual beliefs of the Romano-British.

Curse tablets were a means of controlling the world by relatively simple means, and the writers of these tablets used the same strategies to influence

---

[11] Rodney Legg, *Romans in Britain* (London: Heinemann, 1983), 144. The 2500 inscriptions refer to the *Roman Inscriptions in Britain*, or *RIB*, the most complete collection of Romano-British inscriptions.

[12] Alan K. Bowman, *The Roman Writing Tablets from Vindolanda* (London: British Museum Publications, 1983), 18.

[13] Graham Webster, *The Roman Invasion of Britain* (London: Routledge, 1980), 17. Despite the increased use of the internet to disseminate the small finds of Britain, older finds are still often found only in the back rooms of small museums and have yet to be published or publicized.

[14] Lindsay Allason-Jones, "The Family in Roman Britain," in *A Companion to Roman Britain*, ed. Malcolm Todd (Malden, MA: Blackwell Publishing, 2004) 274; Lindsay Allason-Jones, *Daily Life in Roman Britain* (Oxford: Greenwood World Publishing, 2008), 135; and Marilynne E. Raybould, *A Study of Inscribed Material from Roman Britain: An Inquiry into Some Aspects of Literacy in Romano-British Society* (Oxford: Archaeopress, 1999), 34ff.

deities as the priests utilized. The curse tablets were mostly sheets of lead, inscribed with a combination of names, magical words, and entreaties to gods and spirits, which were deposited in graves or springs. The intended result was to bind or control people.[15] The elements of curse tablets, such as language, material, and invoked deities, are all meaningful, and when analyzed together we get a fuller sense of popular spiritual beliefs and the everyday needs and wishes of those in antiquity.

Curse tablets have only occasionally been of interest to scholars. The first tablet was published in 1846.[16] Curse tablets were found relatively often, but they were rarely published. Many remained in collections for decades before being published, and many more have yet to be published.[17] Generations of scholars viewed them as being unimportant, uninteresting, and dismissed them as being "of servile origin" since they were personal, unorthodox, and often contained numerous errors, both in grammar and spelling.[18] However, thanks to a newfound interest in the subject of magic and the religious and social information contained within the tablets, the publication and analysis of the tablets has increased dramatically in the last twenty years. Currently over 1600 curse tablets have been discovered, around 500 of which are in Latin, and almost 200 from Roman Britain.[19] The unusually large proportion of curse tablets found in Britain can shed considerable light on the Romano-Britons.

While magic manuals provided a formula to be used by the curse writer, there was room for individualization, which is why curse tablets are possibly the best tool to understanding popular spiritual beliefs in the Roman Empire. The information contained in these tablets can often be revealing about the personal lives and society of the petitioner. The proliferation and universality of the use of curse tablets indicates how closely the Mediterranean and Western Europe were interconnected, both intellectually and religiously, during the millennium that curse tablets were used. The tablets showed uniformity in their formulae, which revealed that the cultures which used the tablets considered the same set of elements to be crucial in communicating to the divine realm. The breadth of

---

[15]Andrew J. Bayliss, "Curse-Tablets as Evidence: Identifying the Elusive 'Peiraikoi Soldiers,'" *Zeitschrift für Papyrologie und Epigraphik* 144 (2003): 125.

[16] David Jordan, "'Remedium Amoris,' a Curse from Cumae," *Mnemosyne*, 4th series, 56, Fasc. 6 (2003): 666.

[17] Alexander Hollmann, "A Curse Tablet from the Circus at Antioch," *Zeitschrift für Papyrologie und Epigraphik* 145 (2003): 67.

[18] A. D. Fraser, "The Ancient Curse: Some Analogies," *The Classical Journal* 17, no. 8 (1922): 457-8.

[19] Bengt Ankarloo and Stuart Clark, ed. *Witchcraft and Magic in Europe: Ancient Greece and Rome* (Philadelphia: University of Pennsylvania Press, 1999), 3.

social status that used curse tablets is also staggering. While the authors of these tablets rarely give their names, let alone professions, they referred to their political and business adversaries, which suggest they held similar positions in society. Named adversaries include a butcher, councilors, a net-maker, shopkeepers, goldsmiths, a pipe maker, a bronze worker, prostitutes, and a physician's assistant, along with names that come from both elite and servile classes, foreigners, and slaves.[20]

Figure 1 - Curse Tablet, image courtesy of the British Museum

Many of the lead curse tablets that give insight into ancient popular beliefs have survived partially intact, although some have been found that are beyond repair.[21] Many have been found in sacred springs, such as in Bath, often in large quantities. The spring at Bath alone contained around 130 curse tablets.[22] Corrosion is often a problem, especially with the nails that invariably are driven through the lead tablet, in order to metaphorically nail down a person's will.[23]

---

[20]John G Gager, ed. *Curse Tablets and Binding Spells from the Ancient World* (New York: Oxford University Press, 1992), 131, 137, 142, 143, 155, 157, 158, 163, 164, and 171.

[21] Bengt Ankarloo and Stuart Clark, ed. *Witchcraft and Magic in Europe: Ancient Greece and Rome*, 4.

[22] J. N. Adams, "British Latin: The Text, Interpretation and Language of the Bath Curse Tablets," *Britannia* 23 (1992):1.

[23] For an example: Marit Jentoft-Nilsen, "A Lead Curse Tablet," *The J. Paul Getty Museum Journal* 8 (1980): 199.

The characteristics of the water and the acidity in soil are contributing factors to their survival.[24]

There is occasionally a way to detect if a binding spell or curse tablet has been used, even if it is never found. When a spell to return property was successful, the supplicant often gave a gift as payment to the god who retrieved the goods.[25] Votive offerings in temples often included inscriptions that refer to the fulfillment of vows.[26] Sometimes these inscriptions hint that there was a returned item or fulfillment of a binding spell which was the cause for the vow. These include persons calling upon a god of violence or vengeance that would have no obvious reason to do so, such as a settled family who are thanking the god of war.[27]

Thanks to the survival of so many of these curse tablets, we know much more about both the popular spiritual beliefs and the everyday desires of people in the ancient world. Some scholars have even successfully used curse tablets to fill in gaps in historical knowledge. A. J. Bayliss used a curse tablet to help better understand the *Peiraikoi* soldiers who mysteriously appeared in Attica around 300 B.C.E.[28] Undoubtedly, curse tablets that have yet to be uncovered or published will tell us more about the people and events of the ancient Mediterranean and Roman Empire.

From the curse tablets that have been discovered in Britain, it is clear that the British adapted this Greco-Roman practice to fit their own needs and beliefs. The curse tablets found in Britain are different from other provinces as they are almost all found in water, very few have nails through them, and they are almost all concerned with some sort of theft. These local adaptations are surprising, both in how they are radically different from other provinces, and how they are similar within the province. Since the majority of the curse tablets were found in Bath, a highly Romanized town with a large immigrant population, the trend in curse tablets also suggests that the British method of making curse tablets became the standard in Roman Britain, even amongst the Romans.

The first chapter of this book will survey the historiography of Romano-

---

[24] Ulick R. Evans, *An Introduction to Metallic Corrosion* (New York: St. Martin's Press, 1963), 55 and 72.

[25] A.R. Burn, *The Romans in Britain: An Anthology of Inscriptions* (Oxford: Basil Blackwell, 1964), 50.

[26] R. G. Collingwood, *Roman Inscriptions and Sculptures Belonging to the Society of Antiquaries of Newcastle Upon Tyne* (Newcastle-Upon-Tyne: Northumberland Press, 1929), 16 and 28.

[27] Collingwood, *Roman Inscriptions and Sculptures Belonging to the Society of Antiquaries of Newcastle Upon Tyne*, 16.

[28] These soldiers gained control of Peiraieus and aided Lachares in becoming tyrant there. Andrew J. Bayliss, "Curse-Tablets as Evidence: Identifying the Elusive 'Peiraikoi Soldiers,'" 126ff.

British social history and the problems inherent in studying the subject. The second chapter reviews the practice of creating curse tablets in the Greek and Roman world in order to compare the conventions of the Mediterranean against the Romano-British constructs. The third chapter reviews the religious institutions in Roman Britain, which are not always tied to the real spiritual life of Romano-Britons, which are investigated in chapter four. The fifth chapter discusses the practical reasons for the tablets and what they can contribute to the study of the physical world of Roman Britain.

The curse tablets of Britain show that Romanization was a complex process, which affected the physical world of the Britons, and to a lesser extent, the spiritual world of the Britons. The Romano-Britons adapted the practice of using curse tablets because it coalesced with their worldview, but they rejected certain aspects and added their own twist on this classical practice. Combining the information gleamed from the curse tablets with other information gives us a greater understanding of how the Romano-Britain lived, from what possessions they treasured to what powers they believed their deities possessed.

Chapter 1: The Problem of "Roman Britain"

There are two sides to Roman Britain, the British side and the Roman . . . To a person who approaches it simply from the point of view of England, the Roman period seems an isolated and somewhat unintelligible episode in the history of our country. . . In a history of Rome, it cuts a slightly better figure, because, from this point of view, Roman Britain does form part of the Roman Empire as an organic whole. But it is an uninteresting part. . . . From both these points of view, Roman Britain appears as a dull and meaningless fragment of history. But the real fault is in the points of view.[29]

The field of Romano-British studies is, and always has been, dominated by the English. After Roman troops left Britain, the only historians interested in the Roman occupation of Britain appeared to be the inhabitants of England. In recent decades, scholars from other regions, notably America, Wales, and Scotland, have written on Roman Britain, yet they are still the minority. In some respects the domination by English historians is beneficial, since the evidence is readily available for them. However, there was a long tradition of using Romano-British history for English nationalistic propaganda, and there is also a lot of baggage that is attached to the study of Roman Britain. Therefore, many historians are held captive by their heritage and often write pro or anti Roman polemics, depending on their own background.[30]

The ancient literary works on Britain were created exclusively by upper class Romans and Greeks, who had as much baggage as modern writers, and the sources are often misunderstood. Julius Caesar's comments on the Celtic Gauls have often been applied to the British, especially on the subject of religion.[31] Since there is a lack of sources from the pre-conquest period, his words have been analyzed and reproduced *ad nauseam*, out of sheer necessity. Yet it is highly unlikely that Caesar's descriptions were accurate, and even accurate descriptions of the Celtic Gauls could not necessarily be said to apply to the Britons. Caesar's political agenda dominated his writings, and using religious justification in

---

[29] R. G. Collingwood, *Roman Britain* (Oxford: Clarendon Press, 1966), 1-2.

[30] The works of Martin Henig and Miranda Green come to mind, with Henig generally portraying the Romans as welcome innovators, while Green has often portrayed the Romans as destroying the Celtic culture that flourished. While neither of the authors distorts the facts, they both have strong view on the Romans and Celts that lay at the heart of their often ingenious and influential works.

[31] Gaius Julius Caesar, *Gallic War Book VI*, ed. by E.S. Shuckburgh (Cambridge: Cambridge University Press, 1950) 6.13-17.

conquering Celts was clearly a part of his plan.[32] Therefore, tales of Druids and cannibalism are most likely distorted, if not completely false. Other information held the possibility of being accurate, but many of his statements have been proven to be false.[33]

Tacitus alludes to a large liturgy of works on Britain, yet few sources have come down to us.[34] Tacitus' work is the most helpful and complete of all the Roman sources. Tacitus describes Britain and the initial takeover of the island by the Romans in both the *Annals* and *Agricola*. His comments mostly pertain to the military battles that occurred in the first century C.E., but there were also descriptions of the Britons in this early era of Roman domination. His characterization of the Britons has proved to be more truthful than other ancient historians, yet they can not be said to be completely accurate because he intended not only to describe the British, but critique the Romans at the same time. He saw Romans as servants to their vices, and portrayed the native Britons as "noble savages" of sorts, who were seduced into mimicking decadent Roman ways.[35]

From the early seventeenth century through to the Victorian era, English historians focused on Rome's contributions to English civilization. Rome was civilized, and they bestowed the gift of civilization upon the peoples of ancient England, but not those of Scotland and Ireland. This view of history was helpful in justifying not only the English domination of the British Isles, but their later colonial mission.[36] Along with their imperialistic motives, many historians through the early twentieth century ignored or misread data. Archeology was in its infancy, so the Roman authors were seen as the sources of all information. Even in the nineteenth century, historians believed that Stonehenge could not have been built before the Roman conquest, because none of the Roman authors mentioned it.[37]

Historians of the early twentieth century were not much better. Romano-British histories emphasized the Roman side of the equation, never suggesting that the native population had anything to add to the Roman Empire. F.

---

[32] J. P. V. D. Balsdon, "The Veracity of Caesar," 19ff.

[33] Balsdon's article "The Veracity of Caesar" overviews some of Caesar's work where there is evidence disproving that his writings are false. In the case of Britain and Gaul there is very little definitive evidence to prove his works fallacious or true, and therefore working with his writings should be done with extreme caution.

[34] Tacitus, *Agricola*, 10.1-4.

[35] Tacitus, *Agricola*, 21.4.

[36] Richard Hingley, *The Recovery of Roman Britain 1586-1906: A Colony so Fertile* (Oxford: Oxford University Press, 2008), 326.

[37] Aubrey Burl, *Prehistoric Avebury*, 61.

Haverfield, in his 1906 work, *The Romanization of the Empire,* stated:

> *The lands which the legions sheltered were not merely blessed with quiet. They were also given a civilization, and that civilization had time to take strong root. Roman speech and manners were diffused; the political franchise was extended; city life was established; the provincial populations were assimilated in an orderly and coherent culture. A large part of the world became romanized.*[38]

Similarly, the only Romano-British works deemed worthy of exhibition in the British Museum were classical in style.[39] Throughout the period of the British Empire, it was critical to display the positive side of imperialism, which most historians did with gusto.

R. G. Collingwood was the first well-known historian to value the contributions of the Britons in the development of Romano-British culture. His tireless work in promoting epigraphic and archeological data as the basis for Romano-British studies redefined the field. His best know work was *The Roman Inscriptions in Britain,* or *RIB,* which was an enormous compendium of all the Roman epigraphic finds in Britain. In his other works he was outspoken in his opposition to the old methodologies and ideologies of Romano-British scholars. In 1923's *Roman Britain,* Collingwood objects to looking at Roman Britain from either a purely Roman or British standpoint. He perceived that the Romanization of Britain was not intended to create a radical change in the essential character of the native Britons, and gave the Empire credit for its cosmopolitan nature and ability to embrace numerous cultures.[40]

Later in his career he became increasingly hostile towards the Romans, favoring the native British culture. He portrayed the conquest of Britain as the destruction of beautiful and simple culture, much in the way that Tacitus had. Collingwood even described a pre-Roman British artist as "a child in the portrayal of nature."[41] Most modern scholars tend to dismiss Collingwood due to his radically British bent. Certainly, he was a man of his time, and some of his opinions were influenced by his revulsion to the fascism and imperialism

---

[38] F. Haverfield, *The Romanization of Britain,* 4th edition (Westport, Conn: Greenwood Press, 1979), 11.

[39] H. B. Walters, *Catalogue of the Silver Plate (Greek, Etruscan and Roman) in the British Museum* (London: Trustees of the British Museum, 1921), 1ff.

[40] R. G. Collingwood, *Roman Britain,* 7-9.

[41] R. G. Collingwood, R. G. and J. N, L. Myres, *Roman Britain and the English Settlements,* 2nd ed. (Oxford: Clarendon Press, 1937), 254.

rampant at the time.[42] However, he was the first notable historian to praise the native Britons instead of the Roman conquers, and his work helped bring greater balance to later works.

Since Collingwood's day, historians have attempted to bridge the gap between some of Collingwood's more radical pro-British works and the histories that were imbued with a deep reverence for classical culture. Many major works of the last half century were created by those who were, at heart, classicists such as Martin Henig. The native Britons have been incorporated into the work of these Roman scholars, but they ultimately are looking at Britain from a Roman point of view. Some scholars have rebelled against this Romano-centric history, emphasizing the British point of view, much in the way that Collingwood did in his later work. Both extremes show an inaccurate picture of Roman Britain, but most of the modern Romano-British scholars are able find middle ground and add to our understanding of Roman Britain.

Romano-British historians who emphasize the Roman side of the equation are able to describe how the Romans dealt with a radically different culture that they now held dominion over. Anthony Birely's field of expertise is Roman government and statistical analysis of names. Birely focused on names recorded in Britain and showed that the diverse make-up of the Roman Empire was reflected in the inhabitants of Britain. Yet his work reflected more upon the Romans in Britain than Roman Britain as a whole. This was due in part to the lack of sources which didn't allow for a "systematic study of the various strata in the population."[43] Martin Henig is one of the most popular Roman-British historians. In his various writings about art, religion, and politics he acknowledged that the Celtic spirit was not easily vanquished by Roman culture and society.

The lack of evidence from Roman Britain, coupled with a background in the Classics, can often make even the best scholar make far fetched guesses and give circular arguments. In searching for elusive evidence into the lives of Romano-Britain many scholars look at tombstones, although they far rarer in Britain than any other province.[44] The surviving tombstones tend to give the impression that Britons quickly acculturated.[45] But this is a circular argument, since the only

---

[42] Martin Henig, *The Art of Roman Britain* (Ann Arbor: The University of Michigan Press, 1995), 14.

[43] Anthony R. Birely, *The People of Roman Britain* (Berkeley: University of California Press, 1980), 12.

[44] Valerie M. Hope, "Word and Pictures: The Interpretation of Romano-British Tombstones" *Britannia* 28 (1997):245.

[45] Joan P. Alcock, "The People," in *A Companion to Roman Britain*, ed. Peter A. Clayton (Oxford: Phaidon, 1980), 70-71.

people who would put up tombstones would be those who were Romanized, as creating tombstones was not a native tradition. Using generalizations and comparisons to try and decipher the few pre-British and Romano-British remains has been tempting for many scholars. Yet this can lead to grossly inaccurate claims and comparisons, such as comparing the Britons to Zulus and claiming that all rulers lead for their own profit.[46]

Historians and archeologists who have specialized in fields within the study of Romano-British history are more apt to stay away from any overriding ideology. These scholars tend to have a more balanced or even slightly pro-British view point, but their small focus makes it possible for them to be more objective than scholars who are dealing with Roman Britain as a whole. These scholars work on subjects such as religion (i.e. Miranda Green), textiles (i.e. Wild), or even particular sites (i.e. Cunliffe). However, these specialists rarely write books about Roman Britain as a whole, so the reading public is confronted with books that primarily give an account of Roman Britain from a Classicist's point of view.

Greg Woolf's work on the Romanization of Gaul has been influential to the study of all Roman provinces. Woolf's greatest achievement was to prove that no one was forced to be Roman, and that individuals could decide for themselves which aspects of the Roman culture they chose to have in their lives.[47] Romanization does not mean the dominance of one culture over another, but the creation of a new culture.[48] Furthermore, since there was no definitive Roman culture, there was no one way to be Roman.[49] Woolf gauged the Romanization in Gaul mainly by evaluating economic factors, specifically the trade of common Roman goods, the creation of villas and villa economies, and the expansion of urbanization. While these elements are a good gauge of the culture, they do not explain the process of Romanization, nor do they show how the average Gaul thought or felt.

While the lack of epigraphic evidence inhibits the ability of historians to accurately portray the interplay between native British and Roman cultures, historians have long battled over the correct interpretation of the scant evidence. When considering remains deemed Romano-British, historians tend to emphasize one of these cultures over the other. Problematically, their

---

[46] Neil Faulkner, *The Decline and Fall of Roman Britain* (Stroud, UK: Tempus Publishing, 2004), 71-72.

[47] Greg Woolf, *Becoming Roman: The Origins of Provincial Civilization in Gaul* (Cambridge: Cambridge University Press, 1998), 245.

[48] Greg Woolf, "Beyond Romans and Native" *World Archaeology* 28, no. 3 (1997): 347.

[49] Woolf, *Becoming Roman*, 7.

interpretation does not always have a basis in the data, but their pre-conceived notions of Roman Britain. Since this bias appears in some manner in the majority of works, even archeological reports, it is necessary to highlight the problem through one well documented example.

The temple of Sulis Minerva in Bath, built as early as the 60s C.E., is one of the best documented archeological sites of Roman Britain, primarily because it is the most intact Romano-British temple in Britain.[50] In 1790 the pediment of the temple was found partially intact, the center of which is the much analyzed 'Gorgon' head.[51] Despite the fact that two very similar 'gorgon' heads exist in Chester and Caerleon, the Bath head has invited the most commentary and controversy.[52] The 'gorgon' head is like a Rorschach test for historians. They see what they want to see in it. For some it is proof of the Romanization of the British countryside, for others it is evidence that Celtic sensibilities never disappeared, even in a Roman temple.

Figure 2 - The Bath 'Gorgon' head of the Temple of Sulis Minerva, image courtesy of Mark Bradley

Until the twentieth century, the 'gorgon' head was seen as a classical piece of artwork. The masculine features, including the highly visible mustache and beard, were dismissed as being the result of a "misunderstanding" between the artist and patron.[53] Collingwood and Myres saw the inherent contradiction of a

---

[50] T. F. C. Blagg, "The Date of the Temple of Sulis Minerva at Bath," *Britannia* 10 (1979):103 and Guy de la Bèdoyère, *Roman Britain: A New History* (New York: Thames & Hudson, 2006), 237.

[51] I. A. Richmond and J. M. C. Toynbee, "The Temple of Sulis-Minerva at Bath," *The Journal of Roman Studies* 45 (1955): 99.

[52] Anne Ross, *Pagan Celtic Britain: Studies in Iconography and Tradition* (London: Routledge and Kegan Paul, 1967), 91.

masculine Gorgon. For them, it was a vestige of British culture that had survived and found a place in a Roman temple:

> From the Roman point of view, the Gorgon head is merely one feature of the shield, and the shield is merely an accessory of the divine figure that holds it. On the Bath pediment the Gorgon is the centre of interest, glaring, ferocious, apostrophic, like the human or demonic masks of early La Tène art. Like them, it is male, not female as a Gorgon should be; its beard and moustaches are tangled with the snakes of its own hair; and the rendering of its features, which is wholly unlike anything Roman, recalls in unmistakable detail the same Celtic originals. Romano-British religious syncretism had asked for a Gorgon; the Celtic sculptor responded by supplying a mask whose ancestry is sought for in vain among the Gorgons of Hellenistic and Roman tradition, but can be found at once when we turn to the history of Celtic art.[54]

Collingwood and Myer were able to perceive the British elements of the Bath 'gorgon' head. They saw the problem with identifying the face as that of a Gorgon, since it was male and had an abundant amount of hair. Collingwood and Myer were apt to credit the artist, who they assumed was Celtic, with bridging the gap between the two cultures and giving the 'gorgon' head meaning that it had never had before. The story is one of resistance and perseverance in an age of cultural domination.

Richmond, Toynbee, and de la Bèdoyère also saw the conflation of cultures, but decided that the 'gorgon' was in fact intended to be a gorgon. It was just a gorgon that the native Celtic population could understand along with the Romans.[55] Anne Ross saw the head as an anthropological artifact, an echo of an era long ago. The 'Gorgon heads' of Roman Britain were evidence of the Indo-European heritage that the Britons and Romans shared:

> Placed on temple porticos, eaves of buildings, and shields, in the same contexts as those in which the Celtic 'tête coupée' was exhibited, the symbol of the Gorgon head shared with the Celtic heads in apostrophic powers, but had lost the divine association of the Celtic heads. Celtic heads, frequently horned, were often associated with thermal waters and with the sacred serpent. The Medusa heads likewise tended to be linked with healing springs,

---

[53] F. Haverfield and H. Stuart Jones, "Some Representative Examples of Romano-British Sculpture," *The Journal of Roman Studies* 2 (1912): 134.

[54] Collingwod and Myres, *Roman Britain and the English Settlements*, 255

[55] Richmond and Toynbee, "The Temple of Sulis," 102 and de la Bèdoyère, *Roman Britain*, 236.

while their serpent associations are constant. In this respect, the assimilation of classical to native imagery is a simple matter. The native could clearly make concessions to the classical Gorgon-type, while retaining the symbolism and significance of the divine head, making the symbol acceptable to Roman and native alike. Deeply indigenous native cults could thus be comfortably masked under the image of Medusa, only the individuality of expression, the vigour of execution and the male sex of the heads betraying their non-classical origin.[56]

When scholars who were well versed in Celtic art analyzed the 'gorgon' head, they saw many characteristics of pre-Roman art. The Britons had few pieces of representational art, especially the human form, but the few human figures that they did have were almost exclusively concerned with the head.[57] The head of a human was the source of their power, and heads, both real and figurative, had great meaning to the Britons. Few Celtic gods were represented in human form, but Cernuunos was a notable exception. He was depicted as a human with stags antlers and horns or ram-headed serpents by the fourth century B.C.E.[58] Despite the prominence of Cernuunos' head in pre-Roman iconography, few scholars have suggested that the 'Gorgon head' is not Medusa at all, but a Celtic deity.

In Martin Henig's earlier works he did not mention any Celtic influence in the Bath head, stating that it was Neptune's head which was conflated with Medusa.[59] This is similar to John Hind's later suggestion that it was the Classical deity Oceanus which was being depicted.[60] Later Henig stated that "the pediment is fundamentally Roman in design," but he notes the Celtic features of the head.[61] He deduces that the head was derived from Celtic masks, especially with the "treatment of the eyes, which are lentoid in form with circular pupils."[62] Not only did Henig see this contradictory figure as appealing to both Roman and Celtic traditions, but incorporating both solar and aquatic features, making it a

---

[56] Ross, *Pagan Celtic Britain*, 90.

[57] Graham Webster, *Celtic Religion in Roman Britain* (Totown, NJ: Barnes & Noble Books, 1986), 40.

[58] Valerie J. Hutchinson, *Bacchus in Roman Britain: The Evidence for His Cult*, vol. 1 (Oxford: B.A.R., 1986), 114-115.

[59] Martin Henig, "Roman Religion and Roman Culture" in *A Companion to Roman Britain*, ed. Malcolm Todd (Malden, MA: Blackwell Publishing, 2004), 223.

[60] John Hind, "Whose Head on the Bath Temple-Pediment?" *Britannia* 27 (1996): 358-360.

[61] Henig, *The Art of Roman Britain*, 40.

[62] Henig, *The Art of Roman Britain*, 39.

meaningful and symbolic relief.[63]

Figure 3 - Celtic Relief, image courtesy of Mark Bradley

Barry Cunliffe, the foremost expert on Roman Bath has come to a conclusion on the matter with which many scholars agree. On the superficial level is a Medusa, but a male, Celtic version of a Medusa.[64] Cunliffe suggests that the Celtic elements represent the union of a male sky god and female water goddess. Therefore, "the head emerges as a symbol of the Celtic spirit of the spring, conflated with the strengths of Minerva, set aloft in the heavens dominating all."[65]

The temple and the pediment are certainly classical in style, and it seems logical that the central figure of the pediment would also be classical. Yet this was a classical temple far from the classical world, and the vast majority of the population surrounding the temple would not have understood or responded to classical iconography. The 'Gorgon head' was not created to be a Gorgon, but the head of the Celtic deity Cernuunos. Romans could have seen it as a modified Gorgon, but the Celtic Britons would have seen a deity that knew and understood. The sculptor was almost certainly Celtic, although not necessarily a native Briton, since the depiction of Cernuunos showed a complete understanding into how the god was previously portrayed. The temple itself is often referred to as Romano-British, and the pediment is just that, Roman in

---

[63] Miranda Aldhouse-Green, "Gallo-British Deities and their Shrines," in *A Companion to Roman Britain*, ed. Malcolm Todd (Malden, MA: Blackwell Publishing, 2004), 202.

[64] Barry Cunliffe, "The Sanctuary of Sulis Minerva at Bath: A Brief Review," in *Pagan Gods and Shrines of the Roman Empire*, ed. Martin Henig and Anthony King (Oxford: Oxford University Committee for Archaeology, 1986), 6.

[65] Cunliffe, "The Sanctuary of Sulis Minerva at Bath," 8.

form, Celtic in iconography.

The debate over the 'Gorgon head' demonstrates how historians are still grappling with the concept of Romanization. Much of the recent scholarship on Rome has not been on the eternal city itself, but the provinces. At issue is the relationship between the metropole and periphery and how 'Roman' the Roman Empire really was. This question has been answered, for most of mainland Europe, using economic and epigraphic sources created by the Roman elite. The Romanization of the common man and woman is difficult to ascertain, as is Romanization in one of the most remote provinces, Britain. Using an underutilized source, the curse tablets of Roman Britain, some insight can be given into the extent of Romanization in Britain.

The term Romanization has been ascribed many meanings. While the word has been used for over a century by historians, there is no certain definition. Does it imply that cultures take on aspects of only the central Italian peninsula? Or does it mean that by the first century, when the conquest of Britain occurred, that ideas from around the Empire infiltrated the newly conquered peoples' way of thinking? Did the flow of culture and ideas only flow from the metropole to the periphery? Scholars are apt only to point out the culture that the Romans took from the Greek East, where urban civilization had flourished for millennia before the Empire. Had not the West anything to contribute to the culture of the Empire? Romanization is clearly an ambiguous term.

Woolf warns that Romanization can hold the same connotations as westernization and globalization.[66] Yet Romanization should in no way be conceived of as being akin to conformity. Even before the end of the Roman Republic, Roman no longer meant Italian.[67] Early in Rome's history, after the victory of Rome over Tusculum, Rome allowed Tusculum's residents to become Roman citizens instead of annexing the city. From this point on, Rome became more than a city. Rome was anywhere there were Roman citizens. The lack of clear political and social boundaries allowed Roman culture to become intertwined with local cultures. By the first century C.E. there was no dominant Roman culture since there was a multiplicity of cultures contained with the Roman Empire.[68] Since there was no singular Roman culture, Romanization was not simple acculturation. Romanization consisted of cultural changes that made

---

[66] Woolf, "Beyond Romans and Natives," 339.

[67] Birely, *The People of Roman Britain*, 11-12

[68] Simon Keay, "Innovation and Adaptation: The Contribution of Rome to Urbanism in Iberia," in *Social Complexity and the Development of Towns in Iberia: From the Copper Age to the Second Century AD*, ed. Barry Cunliffe and Simon Keay (Oxford: Oxford University Press, 1995), 299-300.

an area similar to other areas in the Roman Empire, which helped create on overriding Roman culture which nurtured localized diversity.[69]

While many scholars have looked at archaeology for economic proof of Romanization in the provinces, this can only give us a superficial view of society in the provinces. After all, American inspired goods proliferate world-wide, but that does not indicate that the rest of the world has the same politics, beliefs, or society as America. An understanding of the beliefs and society of the Roman provinces is necessary to see if Roman culture penetrated deeper than the physical. Along with the archeological indicators of a shift in culture, less traditional sources should be used to find the historic implications of Romanization.[70]

Romanization meant something different for every province. For instance, Africa had large estates in the style of Roman estates, and much of the work in Romanizing occurred through these economic entities, while urban Romanization was less uniform.[71] Romanization started to occur in Britain long before Britannia became a province. Roman goods and art gained popularity with the elites of southern England in the late Iron Age.[72] The Romanization of Iberia, which in many ways reflected Britain in the variety of cultures before Roman conquest, occurred haphazardly for the first two centuries.[73] In Iberia, like Britain, the number of immigrants was small, but the culture adjusted nonetheless.[74] Native Iberian elites voluntarily became moderately Romanized during the Republican period, but only in the Augustan age was there any indication that they were attempting to be like Roman nobles by patronizing Roman temples.[75] Romanization did not occur equally across Britain, the northern areas not being as Romanized as the southern regions.[76]

Roman Britain has been perceived in many different ways, often dependent

---

[69] Woolf, *Becoming Roman*, 7.

[70] Keay, "Innovation and Adaptation," 291.

[71] T. R. S. Broughon, Broughton, *The Romanization of African Proconsularis* (Baltimore: Johns Hopkins Press, 1929), 157 ff. and David J. Mattingly and R. Bruce Hitchner. "Roman Africa: An Archaeological Review" *The Journal of Roman Studies* 85 (1995): 186.

[72] Henig, *The Art of Roman Britain*, 27.

[73] Keay, "Innovation and Adaptation," 295.

[74] Keay, "Innovation and Adaptation," 298-299.

[75] William E. Mierse, *Temples and Towns in Roman Iberia: The Social and Architectural Dynamics of Sanctuary Design from the Third Century B. C. to the Third Century A. D.* (Berkeley: University of California Press, 1999), 121-122.

[76] David Shottler, *Roman Britain*, 2nd ed. (London: Routledge, 2004), 77.

on the prejudices and specialties of the scholar that is describing it. The influence of Romanization, the positive or negative impact of the Romanization upon Britain, and even the term Romanization itself is often debated. While no scholar can pretend to be free of prejudices, assigning moral judgments to the impact of Rome on Britain should be left to the reader, not the author. To the Britons, Romanization was the combining of the plurality of "Roman" cultures with their native traditions, but only in ways which they found permissible.

Chapter 2: Magic and Curse Tablets in the Roman World

Do you hear, you who so rashly accuse the art of magic? It is an art acceptable to the immortal gods, full of all knowledge of worship and of prayer, full of piety and wisdom in things divine, full of honor and glory since the day when Zoroaster and Oromazes established it, high-priestess of the powers of heaven.[77]

Curse tablets are very complex documents that contain layers of symbolism. In order to understand how and why curse tablets differ from location to location, it is important to understand their theoretical underpinnings. Words, both magical and mundane, were put upon a piece of lead and deposited in the Earth or water in order to persuade spirits and deities to grant favors. These favors ranged from protection to control of others to justice.

Curse tablets are usually labeled as magic by both ancient sources and modern scholars. As Apuleius's defense of magic indicates, most ancient sources were hostile towards magic, either because of the threat that magic posed or because of the belief that magicians were charlatans. Plato, for one, advocated harsh penalties for anyone practicing necromancy or creating curse tablets.[78] Magic was often associated with deviance and sometimes criminal activity.[79] The Roman legal definition of magic changed over time, and curse tablets were never explicitly forbidden by Roman law, although the Twelve Tables, the oldest surviving Roman law, forbade magic that harmed other citizens.[80]

While harmful magic was despised, helpful rituals that were similar to magic were advocated by prominent Romans. Controlling the natural world by "preternatural means" such as magic words and incantations were not relegated to forbidden magic.[81] Several Latin authors advocated such practices in their works, such as Pliny, who supplied several cures in his writings which involved

---

[77] Apuleius Madaurensis, *Apulei Apologia siue Pro Se de Magia Liber*, ed. H. E. Butler and A. S. Owen (Oxford: Clarendon Press, 1914), 2.1-5. *Auditisne magian, qui eam temere accusatis, artem esse dis immortalibus acceptam, colendi eos ac uenerandi pergnaram, piam scilicet et diuini scientem, iam inde a Zoroastre et Ormaze auctorinus suis nobilem, caelitum antistitam,*

[78] Plato, *Laws*, vol. II, trans. R. G. Bury (Cambridge, MA: Harvard University Press, 1984), 10.909.B-D

[79] William V. Harris, *Ancient Literacy* (Cambridge, M.A.: Harvard University Press, 1989), 127-131.

[80] James B. Rives, "Magic in Roman Law: The Reconstruction of a Crime," *Classical Antiquity* 22, no. 2 (2003): 313-323.

[81] Eugene Tavernner, *Studies in Magic from Latin Literature* (New York, AMS Press, 1966), 8.

symbolic magic.[82] Even the curmudgeonly Cato the Censor advocated using magic words in *De Agri Cultura* to cure a dislocation.[83]

The belief in magic in general and curse tablets in particular is well established for both elites and the general populace. The beliefs associated with magic and curses may have differed between rich and poor, but such deviations can hardly be recorded because of the lack of data from popular sources. Elite sources are often more interested in the literary aspects of magic than a depiction of beliefs, as is shown in literature including witches Medea, Erictho, and Canidia, but there are more earnest depictions of magic earnest.[84] Pliny the Elder, in *Natural History*, wrote at length about the origin and uses of magic and dismisses it as "superstition," yet he wrote on how to repel spells and said everyone feared them, indicating that he himself was not entirely convinced that magic did not exist.[85] Tacitus wrote that the Emperors saw magic and curses as an immediate threat and even attested that the death of Tiberius' heir apparent, Germanicus, was due to a curse.[86]

Curse tablets were known as *defixiones* in Latin, derived from *defigere*, meaning to pin down, and were known as καταδεσμοι in Greek.[87] The tablets were inscribed with spells that bound the will and the body of another person, making the victim obey the spell-caster's orders. The Greeks invented curse tablets, although the concept of written curses was not their own, as cuneiform maledictions are found in contracts dating as far back as the third millennium B.C.E. and written Egyptian curses date from Middle Kingdom.[88] The earliest surviving tablets come from Attica and Sicily, dating from the fifth century B.C.E.[89] The use of curse tablets spread throughout the Greek speaking world

---

[82] Pliny the Elder, *Natural History,* vol. VIII, ed. W. H. S. Jones (London: William Heinemann Ltd., 1963), 28.12.47-28.13.52.

[83] Cato, *De Agri Cultura* (Leipzig: Teveneri, 1895), 160.

[84] Elizabeth Ann Pollard, "Witch-Crafting in Roman Literature and Art: New Thoughts on an Old Image," *Magic Ritual, and Witchcraft* 3, no. 2 (2009): 119-138.

[85] Pliny the Elder, *Natural History,* Vol. VIII, 30.5, 32.14 and 28.4.

[86] Tacitus, *Annals*, 3.13.

[87] Georg Luck, ed., *Arcana Mundi: Magic and the Occult in the Greek and Roman Worlds,* 2nd ed. (Baltimore: John Hopkins University Press, 2006), 48.

[88] Samuel A. B. Mercer, "The Malediction in Cuneiform Inscriptions" *Journal of the American Oriental Society* 34 (1915): 283-392 and Jan Assmann, "When Justice Fails: Jurisdiction and Imprecation in Ancient Egypt and the Near East," *The Journal of Egyptian Archaeology* 78 (1992): 154, & 158.

[89] Matthew W Dickie, *Magic and Magicians in the Greco-Roman World* (London: Routledge, 2003), 48 and Bengt Ankarloo and Stuart Clark, ed., *Witchcraft and Magic in Europe: Ancient Greece and Rome*

and were introduced to the Romans by Greek colonists in Italy. The earliest recovered Roman curse tablet dated from the Augustan era, but they certainly existed before this period.[90] Curse tablets have been discovered all over the Roman Empire and beyond, suggesting that they were as universal as Roman culture itself.

The essential element of a curse tablet was the name or names of those who were to be affected by the curse.[91] Some curse tablets were simply a list of names, especially the earliest Greek tablets, although only fourteen of the British tablets are that basic.[92] Identifying these simple tablets as *defixiones* can be difficult, with only the location and form of the tablet indicating that the lead plate was intended to be a curse endowed with magical properties, such as the two tablets in Leintwardine that consisted of only names, but were placed in the waters of a bathhouse.[93] The name of the victim was often accompanied by their occupation if the curse pertained to business matters ("I bind Mania the shopkeeper"), otherwise it tended to list their relations, especially who their mother was ("Juliana, to whom Marcia gave birth"), although in Britain this was rarely done.[94] There appear to be two reasons for charting descent matrilineal in the tablets. The first is that the mother of a child is certain, while the father of the child is not. The other reason for this was that it was an inversion of the patrilineal society of the Greeks and Romans, and by using matrilineal descent; the writer was therefore eschewing the norms of society, as magic was wont to do.[95] The Britons charted their genealogy differently, which was perhaps why the victims' parents were rarely given.[96]

Verbal spells were most likely used during the creation of a curse tablet which only contained names.[97] Fritz Graf argues that this was the most important element for the creation of the curse tablets, as it was for other spells.[98]

(Philadelphia: University of Pennsylvania Press, 1999), 4. Curse tablets became plentiful in the Greek world in the fourth and third centuries B.C.E., and only waned in popularity after the third century C.E. Jordan, "Contributions to the Study of Greek Defixiones," 4.

[90] Dickie, *Magic and the Occult in the Greek and Roman Worlds*, 128.

[91] H. S. Versnel, "The Poetics of the Magical Charm: An Essay in the Power of Words," in *Magic and Ritual in the Ancient World*, ed. Paul Mirecki and Marvin Meyer (Leiden: Brill, 2002), 112.

[92] Ankerloo and Clark, *Magic and Witchcraft in Europe*, 26.

[93] Appendix I #86 and #87.

[94] Gager, *Curse Tablets and Binding Spells* 157, #62 (first example) and 89, #21 (second example)

[95] Fritz Graf, *Magic in the Ancient World*, trans. Franklin Philip (Cambridge, Mass.: Harvard University Press, 1997), 127-128.

[96] Frederic Seebohm, *The Tribal System in Wales* (London: Longmans, Green & Co., 1895), 73.

[97] Ankerloo and Clark, *Magic and Witchcraft in Europe*, 26.

This spell eventually became a part of the tablet proper. The spell itself, indicated by phrases such as "I bind," "I restrain," or "I curse," is present on most of the tablets that have been recovered from the Mediterranean, although not Britain. Binding was the intended purpose of most of the curse tablets, and therefore the phrase tended to be repeated *ad nauseam*, as in a Syrian tablet that reads ". . . bind his neck, his hands, his feet, bind, bind together. . ."[99]

The ancient connotation of the word "binding" was strongly associated with fixation, which is why many curse tablets were sealed by a nail through the folded or rolled piece of lead.[100] The nail driven through the tablet bound or fixed someone's will. By binding someone, the writer of the curse would have total control of them. The victims were unable to do specific actions and the body parts necessary to do those actions are also bound.[101] Therefore, when Seuthes wanted to make sure his opponents in court could not speak, he bound "the tongue and soul and speech" of said opponents.[102]

The curse writer, even if they were a magician by trade, did not have the power to bind anyone without some supernatural help. There were two main groups that the supplicant addressed in order to achieve his or her goals. The first was the dead. The dead, especially the untimely dead, were agents that were simultaneously powerful and controllable.[103] The dead were able to use the powers of the underworld to torture the living and thus they were often invoked as the instrument of binding in the tablets, as in Greek tablet that promised the dead "If you restrain and constrain them for me, I will honor you and prepare a most agreeable gift for you."[104] The dead were seen as powerful and knowledgeable.[105] The untimely dead and those not buried were restless, and neither fully belonged to the land of the living nor the dead.[106] They haunted the

---

[98] Fritz Graf, "Theories of Magic in Antiquity," in *Magic and Ritual in the Ancient World*, ed. Paul Mirecki and Marvin Meyer (Leiden: Brill, 2002), 94.

[99] Gager *Curse Tablets and Binding Spells,* 53 #4.

[100] R. G. Collingwood and Ian Richmond, *The Archeology of Roman Britain* (London: Methuem & Co., 1930), 371.

[101] Ankerloo and Clark, *Magic and Witchcraft in Europe*, 27.

[102] Gager, *Curse Tablets and Binding Spells*, 132.

[103] Daniel Odgen, *Night's Black Agents: Witches, Wizards, and the Dead in the Ancient World* (London and New York: Hambledon Continuum, 2008), 142.

[104] Gager, *Curse Tablets and Binding Spells*, 138 #48.

[105] Not all ancients believed ghosts had power. According to both Homer and Cicero, only Tiresias the seer was wise in the underworld, all other souls were shadows. Cicero, *De Divinatione* (Stutgardiae: in aedibus B. G. Teubneri, 1965), I.40. *quorum de altero etiam apud inderos Homerus ait 'solum sapere, ceteros umbrarum vagari modo'*

land until the time that they would have died naturally. Some philosophic schools, such as the Pythagoreans and Platonists believed that the dead held special wisdom, and thus, special powers.[107]

Despite their power and wisdom, the dead did not possess a corporeal form and were subject to the will of the magician who had summoned them.[108] Sometimes the curse writer had to threaten the dead or make a deal with them in order that they carry out the binding spell.[109] Some writers offered a gift as a reward, while others bound the spirits by oath.[110] The tablets rarely showed what means the curse writer used to control the spirits, indicating that these stipulations were done verbally. As well as being assistants, the corpses of the spirits summoned also acted as a metaphor for the victims' will and power, as they "lie here idle" and "lie here useless."[111]

While ghosts and spirits were powerful and controllable, gods were far more able to enact out binding spells and therefore were commonly called upon in curse tablets. In the magical manual known as the *Papiri Graciae Magica* or *PGM*, deities were the most popular choice to appeal to for performing spells and curses.[112] The gods of the underworld were the most apt to be called upon. Hermes/Mercury, Persephone/Kore, Hecate, Ge/Gaia, Hades/Pluto and Demeter/Ceres were the deities invoked most often.[113] These gods could be called upon for any sort of spell, drawing upon powers beyond their recognized domains. Therefore, Hermes could cast a love spell and Demeter could insist on justice for the wronged. Because of their exalted status, the deities were called upon in a much more humble manner than the spirits were.[114]

Besides the dead and deities, other spirits were sometimes called upon to aid in spells. In the *PGM*, a constellation which manifests itself as an angel was invoked.[115] Other angels appear in magical texts from the Eastern

---

[106] Daniel Ogden, *Greek and Roman Necromancy* (Princeton: Princeton University Press, 2001), 225.

[107] Odgen, *Greek and Roman Necromancy*, 243-44.

[108] Leda Jean Ciraolo, "Supernatural Assistants in the Greek Magical Papyri," in *Ancient Magic and Ritual Power*, edited by Marvin Meyer and Paul Mirecki (Boston: Brill Academic Publishers, 2001), 286.

[109] Ankerloo and Clark, *Magic and Witchcraft in Europe*, 17.

[110] Gager, *Curse Tablets and Binding Spells*, 138, 62-63.

[111] Gager, *Curse Tablets and Binding Spells*, 131 and 90.

[112] Ciraolo, "Supernatural Assistants in the Greek Magical Papyri," 280.

[113] Ankerloo and Clark, *Magic and Witchcraft in Europe*, 44.

[114] Ankerloo and Clark, *Magic and Witchcraft in Europe*, 44-45.

[115] Ciraolo, "Supernatural Assistants in the Greek Magical Papyri," 285 and Hans Dieter Betz, ed.,

Mediterranean, such as one addressed to "you holy and mighty angels" which dates from around the fourth century, C. E.[116] Most of these appear to be Jewish or Christian curse tablets and spells, but they appear to function in a similar way to their polytheistic counterparts, although they sometimes included verses from the Bible.[117] There was even the occasional curse tablet invoking God Himself.[118] In other tablets there appears to be an amalgam of polytheistic and monotheistic powers that were invoked, with one Greek cursing an opponent "with Hekatean words and Hebrew oaths."[119] While calling upon an array of spirits and gods from around the Mediterranean was not uncommon, this combination of monotheistic and polytheistic spirits was rare. The combination of Greco-Roman, Celtic, Egyptian, and Semitic deities and spirits is remarkable in these tablets, and shows the extent of religious and cultural exchange in the ancient Mediterranean.

Voces mysticae, or magic words, which were presumably spoken during the rites creating the tablets, were used to call upon the gods and spirits to help curse tablets achieve their ends. The earliest surviving appearance of *voces mysticae* in a curse tablet dates from the fourth century B.C.E. in Greece, using what is known as the *Ephesia grammata*, six magic words that reoccur in many tablets, which are *askion, kataskion, lix, tetrax, damnameneus, aision*.[120] Some of the *voces mysticae* were secret names of deities.[121] By using these secret names, the writer of the curse tablet would have more control and direct contact with the deity. The *voces mysticae* were guarded secrets and were one of the reasons that people consulted either experts or magic manuals for the creation of an effective curse tablet. The secret names of deities sometimes invoked deities that were otherwise unknown, but since the *voces mysticae* by definition were meaningless to everyone but the deities, it is difficult to discern how many referred to unknown deities and how many were simply secret names of well known gods.

Other *voces mysticae* were used much like the modern *abracadabra*, as words that had magical powers in themselves, but did not refer to a deity.[122] Such *voces*

The Greek Magical Papyri in Translation (Chicago: University of Chicago Press, 1986), I.42-195.

[116] Gager, *Curse Tablets and Binding Spells*, 94, #26; also see 59, 70, 106, 168, and 170.

[117] Gager, *Curse Tablets and Binding Spells*, 205-207.

[118] Gager, *Curse Tablets and Binding Spells*, 108 and Kimberly B. Stratton, *Naming the Witch: Magic, Ideology, and Stereotype in the Ancient World* (New York: Columbia University Press, 2007), 155-156.

[119] Gager, *Curse Tablets and Binding Spells*, 183-184.

[120] Versnel, "The Poetics of the Magical Charm: An Essay in the Power of Words," 113-114.

[121] Ciraolo, "Supernatural Assistants in the Greek Magical Papyri," 281.

[122] Abracadabra itself was used since 200 CE. See A. Nelson, "Abracadabra," *Eranos* 44 (1946): 326-

mysticae were used in all forms of ancient magic, even those that were used in public, such as in the spell recommended by Cato the Censor for healing a dislocation.[123] The *voces mysticae* may have once had a meaning, the words could have been borrowed from another language, or they may have simply been made up.[124] The obviously made up *voces mysticae* often consist of repeating syllables, which, when spoken, would sound like a chant or poetry. In a similar vein, many of the more elaborate and lengthy curse tablets are written in some form of meter.[125]

Despite these poetic devices, curse tablets remain an excellent indicator of what the non-elite Greco-Roman population wanted. Curse tablets were able to convey the needs and desires of everyday people in the ancient world in a way that few, if any, other artifacts were able to do. Some historians ignore the emotional element to these curse tablets, relegating their studies purely to the mechanics of the tablets, but they are doing their subject matter a disservice. Whether it was a husband asking for vengeance on a cheating wife or a plea for the safe return of a treasured piece of property, there was always a great human need behind the curse tablets. This essential humanity is not only one of the most intriguing elements of the tablets, but it is an otherwise intangible piece of the past. As Daniel Ogden eloquently asserted, "the tablets can, it seems, give us brief flashes of direct access to the unmediated innermost feelings of individuals from the ancient world in a way that it is difficult enough to achieve even in the case of the individuals around us."[126] The only other non-elite literary sources that we have that give us such insight are letters, such as those found in Vindolanda.[127] However, these were meant to be seen by others, making the writer more inhibited in what was written, while the curse tablets were between the author and the deity, and never meant to be seen by human eyes. Curse tablets can show how an individual coped with life on a spiritual level, in a way that they perhaps never showed to the world.

The needs and wishes of those who used curse tablets to achieve their ends were varied, but there were certain categories in which they can be placed in.

336.

[123] Cato, *De Agri Cultra*, 160 and Versnel, "The Poetics of the Magical Charm: An Essay in the Power of Words," 106-107, 118. The words he says to use are *huat hauat huat ista pista sista dannabo dannaustra.*

[124] Versnel, "The Poetics of the Magical Charm: An Essay in the Power of Words," 108.

[125] Versnel, "The Poetics of the Magical Charm: An Essay in the Power of Words," 131.

[126] Odgen, *Night's Black Agents*, 140-141.

[127] Alan K. Bowman, *Life and Letters on the Roman Frontier: Vindolanda and Its People* (New York: Routledge, 1994), 103ff.

Love spells are one of the most intriguing categories, as they can portray the emotions of ancient peoples better than any other category. The curse tablets reveal that the line between love and hate was very close, and some binding spells were more about coercion than love. Many love spells were intended to create great passion in the victim, usually at the expense of the victim's spouse or lover.[128] Pain and madness were the victims' fate until they give themselves into the spell-caster's desires:

> *Lead Euphemia, to whom Dorothea gave birth, to me, Theon, to whom Proechia gave birth, loving me with love, desire, affection, sexual intercourse, and a frenzied love. Cause her limbs, her liver, and her genitals to burn until she comes to me, loving me and not ignoring me.[129]*

This tablet was similar to many others that were created by men who were intent on receiving passionate love, whereas women were more likely to have enduring love as their goal.[130]

Pleas for vengeance, justice, and the return of property were common topics for curse tablets in Britain. The curse writer would ask for justice by putting the stolen object in the care of the god, and the god would presumably want it back: "Silvianus has lost his ring and given half to Nodens. Among those who are called Senicianus do not allow health until he brings it to the temple of Nodens."[131] It appears that Silvianus never recovered his ring, as a gold ring was unearthed nearby, with the words "Seniciaunus, live in God" inscribed on it.[132] Unlike the other curses, theft tablets were often placed in a temple or shrine, most likely because they would be seen by the offending criminal and return the property and turn themselves in. When the object was returned, the god would receive a gift, in this case, Nodens would have received something worth half of what Silvianus' ring was worth. In a world without police, the public plea for justice was often the only recourse for someone who had suffered at the hands of criminals.

Financial competition, wither it was from business or gambling, compelled

---

[128] Christopher A. Faraone, *Ancient Greek Love Magic* (Cambridge, Mass: Harvard University Press, 1999), 41-95.

[129] Gager, *Curse Tablets and Binding Spells*, 105.

[130] Faraone, *Ancient Greek Love Magic*, 146-174.

[131] R.G. Collingwood and R. P. Wright, editors, *The Roman Inscriptions of Britain* I, (Gloucester: Alan Sutton Publishing, 1990), 104.

[132] Collingwood, *Roman Inscriptions of Britain* II #2422.14.

many people to create *defixiones* to bind their competitors. These curses could be among the most vicious, inciting proclamations such as "stab his tongue, and if he is in any way about to do business, may it be unprofitable for him, and may everything be lost, stripped away, and destroyed."[133] These tablets usually cursed not only the financial competitor, but their staff, family, and the place of business itself. Along with traditional businesses, those who were involved with gambling and sports utilized curse tablets, especially when in came to the wildly popular chariot races. Curses were put on horses and riders alike, and have been found everywhere from Carthage to Rome to Antioch.[134] One of the most heated rivalries throughout the Roman Empire was between the chariot factions, and when gambling was added to that competition, the curse tablets must have seemed a necessary safeguard to ensure victory.

Curse tablets binding the speech and will of opponents in legal and political disputes were popular, especially in Greece. Ironically, these appear to have been incredibly prevalent in the world's first democracy, Athens.[135] This suggests that even though everyone was equal under the law, many people tried everything they could to give themselves an unfair advantage. The binding tended to be more specific in these cases than in the other categories; binding the tongue, mouth, and speech was the primary goal of these tablets. The curse writer would bind the "soul and mind and tongue and plans" of their opponent so as to make them utterly incompetent in court.[136] The writer of the curse tablet intended to make not only the plaintiff (it is almost always the defendant who created the curse) but the plaintiff's witnesses mute and/or confused when in court.

The placement of curse tablets once they were finished was crucial, as placing them in the wrong location risked the supernatural powers not receiving the invocation. Therefore, the location used often directly correlated with the gods or powers that were being addressed. Many curse tablets have been found in water, especially sacred springs.[137] These springs were conceived of as being gateways to the underworld, and by placing curse tablets in them there would be direct access to the infernal deities who were so often invoked. Sacred springs

---

[133] Gager, *Curse Tablets and Binding Spells*, 160.

[134] J. E. Lowe, *Magic and Latin Literature* (Oxford: Basil Blackwell, 1929), 17; David Jordan, "A Curse on Charioteers and Horses at Rome," *Zeitschrift für Papyrologie und Epigraphik* 141 (2002): 141; and Hollmann, "A Curse Tablet from the Circus at Antioch," 68ff.

[135] Gager, *Curse Tablets and Binding Spells*, 117-120.

[136] Gager, *Curse Tablets and Binding Spells*, 127.

[137] A good example is found in Marit Jentoft-Nilsen, "A Lead Curse Tablet," 199.

existed all around the Roman Empire, and many have been found filled with curse tablets, proving that the belief in the otherworldliness of springs was universal throughout the Empire. The biggest cache of curse tablets was found in the spring at Bath in England.

The other common location where curse tablets were deposited was in graves, particularly the graves of those who died a violent or untimely death. The curse tablet creators' intent was to initiate contact between the land of the living and the land of the dead, and graves, being inside the Earth and filled with death, were perfect for creating a places neither living nor dead.[138] If the spirit of the dead was being called upon to enact the binding curse, their grave was the ideal place to bury the tablet. Many times the name of the person buried was inscribed on the curse tablet itself, but it is unclear how often the writer knew the person whose spirit they were invoking. It may have been that they waited until they got to the cemetery and found a suitable grave to write who they were addressing.

Curse tablets were also placed where the victim of the curse would have lived and/or worked and at temples.[139] Tablets found buried under a workplace often pertained to commercial disputes and worked to ruin the business and all who worked there. Shops, workshops, and taverns were typically the main targets. Circuses and theaters were also the sites of curse tablet burial for similar reasons, to ruin a competitor's chance to win, thereby guaranteeing victory for the writer of the curse.[140] The placement of tablets at temples was different. As mentioned before, curse tablets condemning criminals were placed in public as a warning to return property, and the placement also allowed the supplication to be heard by the god or goddess.

Throughout the Mediterranean world, curse tablets were primarily made of lead. Lead was specifically referenced as the material for curse tablets in several sections of the *PGM*. Some spells specify using a section of lead piping, while others specify a plate or a building material known as a *lamella*.[141] By some scholars' definitions, such as Fritz Graf's, only curses written on lead may be called curse tablets. There have been several suggestions about why the lead was used in the making of curse tablets. Graf and others have suggested that it was

---

[138] Odgen, *Greek and Roman Necromancy*, 251, 253.

[139] Daniel Odgen, *Magic, Witchcraft, and Ghosts in the Greek and Roman Worlds: A Sourcebook*, 2nd ed. (Oxford: Oxford University Press, 2009), 210.

[140] Eve D'Ambra, "Racing with Death: Circus Sarcophagi and the Commemoration of Children in Roman Italy." *Hesperia Supplements* 41 (2007):348-350.

[141] Betz, *The Greek Magical Papyri in Translation*, 94, 106, and 128.

used because lead was cold to the touch and dull, indicating a connection to the Earth.[142] The tablets themselves refer the lead's similarity to the intended result of the curse, making someone "worthless and cold."[143] This indicates that sympathetic magic was the reason for the selection of lead as the material for curse tablets. A utilitarian reason would be that lead was relatively inexpensive and widely used, as is evident from any catalogue of Greek or Roman artifacts.[144] Lead is also very durable.[145] Due to the cost of metal, it was probably primarily a financial decision, but was justified by the unique aspects of lead which lent them to being endowed with magical associations to the dead and worthless.[146]

Lead may have been the main material for curse tablets, but there were a variety of other metals and materials which were used to create curse tablets, although these materials may not have had the same magical significance that lead had. Pewter may have been used for makeshift curse tablets, and due to its lead content, it would not have stretched the definition of a curse tablet too far.[147] Bronze curse tablets have also been found alongside lead in caches such as the one in Bath.[148] Tin, limestone, talc, and gemstones have also been used.[149] Potsherds and bowls were also used, and sometimes appeared to be the dominant medium used in some times and places, such as the Semitic lands in late antiquity.[150]

While lead may have been the preferred material for curse tablets, there appears to have been a different preferred material for writing on the tablets. In the *PGM* the lead curses were to be inscribed with a bronze stylus.[151] Spells that included writing but were not curse tablets did not specify the material of the writing implement, suggesting that there was either a connection between the lead sheet and bronze stylus or bronze and the act of binding.[152] Styli came in both bronze and iron, but it is unclear why bronze was the only permissible

---

[142] Graf, *Magic in the Ancient World*, 133.

[143] Gager, *Curse Tablets and Binding Spells*, 127.

[144] Collingwood, *Roman Inscriptions of Britain*, Vol. II, Fac. 1, 82-124.

[145] Ankerloo and Clark, *Magic and Witchcraft in Europe*, 10.

[146] Ankerloo and Clark, *Magic and Witchcraft in Europe*, 11.

[147] Collingwood, *Roman Inscriptions of Britain*, Vol. II, Fac. 2, 76.

[148] Richard Broxton Onians, *The Origins of European Thought: About the Body, the Mind, the Soul, the World, Time and Fate* (Cambridge: Cambridge University Press, 1951), 206.

[149] Ankerloo and Clark, *Magic and Witchcraft in Europe*, 10.

[150] Ganger, *Curse Tablets and Binding Spells*, 205-207.

[151] Betz, *The Greek Magical Papyri in Translation*, 128,269, and 274.

[152] Betz, *The Greek Magical Papyri in Translation*, 66 and 94.

material to be used for writing curse tablets.[153]

The method of writing the curse tablets was as important as what was written on them. In addition to the use specific materials, tablets were to be written in a certain way. Many tablets were written with the left hand, in reverse, or partially upside down, as is attested to in both the magical manuals and the tablets themselves.[154] This inversion of normal writing conventions was a part of most magic. Writing with the left hand was doubly significant because it was the reverse of most people's natural tendency, and the left hand, was connected to ill omens throughout the Mediterranean.

In order to create a curse tablet, one had to know the correct spells, both written and verbal, and had to be able to write oneself. Since most people did not have these abilities, some curse tablets were written by professionals, especially in the Greek East.[155] Some of these professionals were undoubtedly very successful, as several caches containing curse tablets that appear to be the work of a single writer have been found, such as those from the well in the agora of Athens.[156] The identity of these professionals is of some debate, as they appear to have used standardized magical formulas and filled in any relevant information when they were hired. Amateur curse writers usually had much more basic tablets with less legible writing and fewer *voces mysticae*, but if they possessed a magical manual or had been given instructions by the professional magicians, their work may have been just as elaborate as a professionally written tablet. Amateurs had more freedom to write what they wished, and these tablets are often the ones that are the most revealing.

The curse tablets of the Greco-Roman world had an extensive history long before they were ever used in Britain. The method of creating and depositing the curse tablets was riddled with symbolic meaning that appeared to transcend the cultural differences of the Mediterranean world. The information contained within the tablets showed intimate details of people's beliefs, needs, and desires. The conventions that were created in the Mediterranean *defixiones* are important to remember when looking at the Romano-British curse tablets, which seem to disregard these conventions in most situations.

---

[153] *Guide to the Antiquities of Roman Britain* (London: The Trustees of the British Museum, 1964), 48.

[154] Versnel, "The Poetics of the Magical Charm: An Essay in the Power of Words," 144.

[155] Dickie, *Magic and Magicians in the Greco-Roman World*, 48.

[156] Dickie, *Magic and Magicians in the Greco-Roman World*, 243.

Chapter 3: The Religious World of the Romano-Britons

. . .a general survey inclines me to believe the Gauls established themselves in an island so near to them. Their religious belief may be traced in the strongly-marked British superstition.[157]

The temples, shrines, and depictions of the gods are all that remain of the Romano-British religion. This religion was utterly unique, different than its parent religious systems, and even different from the culturally similar Romano-Gallic religion. While the religion of the Romano-Britons does not necessarily attest to the deeper beliefs of the Romano-Britons, it was the backdrop for their spiritual beliefs. It is in this context that the curse tablets were created. The changes in the religion of Britain are far better known than the spiritual changes that the Britons encountered, and only with an understanding of Romano-British religion can the details of the curse tablets be understood.

Superficially, Roman religion was quite different than the native Celtic religion of Britain. The Romans had temples, professional diviners, and a hierarchy of priests and priestesses, while the Britons had little to none of these.[158] Yet underneath the structured devotional aspect of Roman religion, the premise of the Romans' religious life was very similar to that of the Celts. They both believed that there were numerous divine forces in nature, and that by gaining their favor, the divine elements could help individuals and the community. Since the religions of the two were similar, they were able to cohabitate, integrate, and even spawn new religious and spiritual phenomena.

There have certainly been a number of historians who have speculated on the evolution of beliefs of the ancient Britons.[159] Since the ancient Britons were not literate and their religion was described solely by outsiders, or after centuries of Roman influence, it is probably impossible to discern the true metamorphosis of British religion. At best, we can look at Romano-British religion to determine what was foreign, what was ancient, and what derived from the interaction between native and foreign beliefs.

British religion was not a coherent religion, per se. The religion in Britain was highly localized, with local rituals, local deities, and local superstitions.[160]

---

[157] Tacitus, *Agricola*, 11.

[158] M. J. T. Lewis, *Temples in Roman Britain* (Cambridge: Cambridge University Press, 1966), 4.

[159] Joan P. Alcock, *Daily Life of the Pagan Celts* (Oxford: Greenwood World Publishing, 2009), 132.

[160] John Wacher, *Roman Britain* (London: J.M. Dent & Sons, 1980), 217.

However, these local variations were similar to one another since the British shared a collective ethnic background, and interaction between tribes was common. Britons respected various taboos, most of which were related to food, while others had to do with moving in the direction of the sun instead of counterclockwise, or widdershins.[161] Status within society and religion were linked. Some religious actions could only be done by those of a certain social ranking.[162] In the insular agricultural societies of pre-Roman Britain, religion and ritual were intertwined with basic social interactions and practices.[163]

Other than the elimination of the Druids, Romans did not attempt to alter the beliefs or practices of the native Britons. Despite the introduction of new practices, structures, and deities, the coming of Rome did not have a substantial impact on British religion.[164] The native Britons held on to many of their religious beliefs, although they were supplemented by Roman religion. They added new elements to the religious make-up of Britain, but they did not eliminate significant practices and beliefs.[165] The Britons clearly choose which elements to incorporate, which is why different tribal areas adopted some gods over others, such as the Cornovii embracing Venus.[166] One inadvertent consequence of the Roman conquest was that Britain gained a more unified concept of religion, since the once fractured regions of Britons now were interacting with one another, politically, economically, and religiously on a level they never did before.[167] Although religion was supplemented, local deities and idiosyncrasies remained.[168]

The Romans considered themselves to be extremely devout and strict adherents to the rites and customs of their ancestors.[169] This stringent observance to ancient ritual compelled them to create temples and colleges of

---

[161] Webster, *Celtic Religion in Roman Britain*, 29-30.

[162] Graham Webster, "What the Britons Required from the Gods as Seen Through the Pairing of Roman and Celtic Deities and the Character of Votive Offerings" in *Pagan Gods and Shrines of the Roman Empire*, ed. Martin Henig and Anthony King (Oxford: Oxford University Committee for Archaeology, 1986), 57.

[163] Colin Haselgrove, "Society and Polity in Late Iron Age Britain" in *A Companion to Roman Britain*, ed. Malcolm Todd (Malden, MA: Blackwell Publishing, 2004), 19.

[164] Webster, *The British Celts and Their Gods Under Rome*, 111.

[165] Wacher, *Roman Britain*, 219.

[166] Miranda J. Green, *The Religions of Civilian Roman Britain* (Oxford: British Archaeological Reports, 1976), 76-85.

[167] Aldhouse-Green, "Gallo-British Deities and their Shrines," 194.

[168] Collingwood and Myres, *Roman Britain and the English Settlements*, 261.

[169] Henig, "Roman Religion and Roman Culture in Britain," 221.

priests that were the same throughout the Empire. While provincials were expected to take part in the occasional rites and rituals of the Roman cults, devotion to these cults and membership in the priesthood was purely voluntary. The majority of provincials celebrated a Roman deity's feast day, but had little other contact with the cult. The most important religious rites were concerned with the regeneration of life and success in agriculture. Italian peasants were probably as apt as British peasants were to focus their religious and ritual energies on the natural world, and the cycle of the season and life. This commonality is why villa mosaics that occur from Tunisia to Britain incorporate similar agrarian deities and symbolism.[170] The religions of the common Roman and Briton were not drastically different.[171]

While the pre-Roman Britons worshipped many spirits and deities, they did not worship them in temples. Unlike Greco-Roman religions, there were no holy spaces that needed to be hidden away from prying eyes. The best Greco-Roman analogy to the British perspective would be the augurs, who created a sacred space, *templum*, in the open.[172] The Britons, like the augurs, had no need for temples to shield the secret and holy away from the public and profane.[173] There were many sacred places in Britain, and these were where rituals occurred. Dozens of ditched enclosures have been uncovered that could have been used as ritual space, although only two have been confirmed by archeological evidence to have been so.[174] Certain trees and groves were also sacred, as attested to by Irish literature.[175] Springs were almost always sacred, along with other water features. The British interactions with the divine were probably simple and centered around agriculture. For the Britons, objects and places prominent in everyday life would have held divine significance.[176]

Roofed temples only came into vogue when Celts interacted with Classical civilizations. The spread of these temples was influenced by the willingness of

---

[170] Roger Ling, "The Seasons in Romano-British Mosaic Pavements," *Britannia* 14 (1983): 16-17 and plate I and David Parrish, "Two Mosaics from Roman Tunisia: An African Variation of the Season Theme," *American Journal of Archaeology* 83, no. 3 (1979): 282 and 284.

[171] Webster, "What the Britons Required from the Gods as Seen Through the Pairing of Roman and Celtic Deities and the Character of Votive Offerings," 57.

[172] Marcus Terentius Varro, trans. Roland Kent, *On the Latin Language*, vol. I, (Cambridge, Mass.: Harvard University Press, 1938), 7.8-7.10.

[173] K. W. Muckelroy, "Enclosed Ambulatories in Romano-Celtic Temples in Britain" *Britannia* 7 (1976): 189.

[174] Lewis, *Temples in Roman Britain*, 5.

[175] Ross, *Pagan Celtic Britain*, 33-34.

[176] Alcock, *Daily Life of the Pagan Celts*, 130.

the local population to adapt their rituals to a Romanized model.[177] Many of these shrines and temples were very crude and simple, made of wood and wickerwork, and therefore little trace of them has been uncovered.[178] Most of the more intricate pre-conquest temples were relegated to the "Belgic" areas that were highly Romanized.[179] Twelve rectangular and four circular shrines and temples have been discovered that predate the Roman invasion.[180] It is unclear if the Britons understood these temples as holy spaces in the same way the Romans had. Within the Greco-Roman temple there were areas of differing holiness, with only certain members of the community allowed into certain areas.[181] We have no indication that the Britons conceived of the temples in this way, they may have borrowed the structure of the temple without accepting the concepts that created it.

Temples in the Classical style predate the Roman invasion by a couple of centuries, but only with the conquest of Britain were monumental temples constructed. The earliest temples were constructed in areas with high concentrations of Roman citizens, such as *coloniae* and *municipia*, trading ports, and large, permanent military bases. The creation of urban temples was in response to the specific needs of nearby inhabitants.[182] Therefore these temples were more likely to be purely Roman, and were less likely to involve nature deities. Urban and military temples had more in common with each other than either of them had in common with rural temples.[183]

In the first century, twenty-five temples were built in the towns and countryside.[184] Rural temples were not always responding to the needs of any large populations or local inhabitants.[185] Some temples were located far from any sizable population and the deity to whom they were dedicated was not

---

[177] Lewis, *Temples in Roman Britain*, 10.

[178] Ross, *Pagan Celtic Britain*, 58.

[179] Lewis, *Temples in Roman Britain*, 11.

[180] P. J. Drury, "Non-Classical Religious Buildings in Iron Age and Roman Britain: A Review" in *Temples, Churches and Religion: Recent Research in Roman Britain*, ed. Warwick Rodwell (Oxford: British Archeological Reports, 1980), 45-55, 64-66.

[181] Roger D. Woodward, *Indo-European Sacred Space: Vedic and Roman Cult* (Urbana and Chicago: University of Illinois Press, 2006), 266.

[182] Lewis, *Temples in Roman Britain*, 129, 139. In both the second and third centuries, when military bases became permanent, about half the temples were built around military areas.

[183] Lewis, *Temples in Roman Britain*, 136.

[184] Lewis, *Temples in Roman Britain*, 139.

[185] Lewis, *Temples in Roman Britain*, 129.

always one revered by a large number of local inhabitants. It can therefore be assumed that many of these rural temples were the remnants of pre-Roman religion. Romanized temples stood in sites that were held to be of religious significance before the conquest.

The rituals of British religion changed along with the structures of religion when Romanization occurred. The ancient religion of Britain included sacrifice, as did the religions of the Greco-Roman world, but the British tradition was notably different. Animal sacrifices were not a significant attribute of Celtic religious practice.[186] The slaughter of animals at the altar increased with contact from the Roman world. Another noticeable absence is the lack of common votive offerings. Items were offered to the gods, but these are almost always found in the water, and due to the expense of the items, it is clear that they were placed there by elites.[187] Any sacrifice or offering that the common Briton gave to the gods was of the perishable variety.

Along with new ways to worship, Roman conquest brought a plethora of new cults and gods. Older concepts of Romanization only allowed for Romano-British cults of Roman, Romano-Celtic, or Eastern origin.[188] This is a gross oversimplification. Roman cults, most importantly the Roman cult of the Emperor, were imported to Britain along with Eastern cults such as Mitheras; Roman deities were combined with native deities to form Romano-Celtic religion, such as Sulis-Minerva. However, Eastern cults also merged with native tradition, and those, in turn, combined with Roman cults. The London hunter god found by Merrifield is an example of this, as it took elements from Apollo, a Celtic god of youth, and a savior god from the easternmost reaches of the Empire.[189] With the exceptions of the cult to the Emperor and Mithraism, the cults that made their way to the shores of Britain became something uniquely Romano-British. The transportation of a cult to Britain without any changes was rare.[190]

The epigraphic sources suggest that there was absorption of British deities into the classical cosmology, yet this only represents the elite, official view of

---

[186] Anthony King, "Animal Remains from Temples in Roman Britain" *Britannia* 36 (2005): 333.

[187] Webster, "What the Britons Required from the Gods as Seen Through the Pairing of Roman and Celtic Deities and the Character of Votive Offerings," 57-58.

[188] Haverfield, *The Romanization of Britain*, 67-68.

[189] Ralph Merrifield, "The London Hunter-God," in *Pagan Gods and Shrines of the Roman Empire*, ed. Martin Henig and Anthony King (Oxford: Oxford University Committee for Archaeology, 1986), 91.

[190] Henig, "Roman Religion and Roman Culture in Britain," 221.

religion and could not have been reflecting the real situation.[191] It is clear that native Britons did not embrace all of the Classical deities. Of the 105 temples with known dedications that Lewis surveyed, only Mars, mostly in his native forms, was found in urban, rural, and military contexts.[192] Along with Mars, Hercules, Silvanus, and Vulcan are the most widely depicted classical gods in Roman Britain.[193] Jupiter in the form of Dolichenus, Mithras, and the Celtic Matres had the most temples in Roman Britain.[194] There was also widespread celebration of the cult of Bacchus.[195] A Romano-Celtic version of Bacchus existed because the non-wine related aspects of his cult were already recognized in some form.[196] Along with the worship of the Classical deities the *genii* of people, places, and groups were worshiped.[197]

The cults of common Roman gods were imported to Britain, but they were not the only deities to cross the channel. Due to the large number of military personnel to be stationed in Britain, the cult of the warrior god Mithras was widespread.[198] Other, more obscure deities, such as the goddess Garmangabis, had devotees in Britain.[199] It is interesting to note which cults did not flourish in Britain. While the cult of Isis was popular around the Empire, there is little evidence of her cult, or the cult of other Egyptian gods in Britain. More surprising is the lack of Gallic deities in Britain. A similar culture and trade had long linked Gaul and Britain, but some of the most popular Gallic gods are barely noted amongst the epigraphy of Britain. The popular horse goddess from Gaul, Epona, was not imported. Only a couple of references to her have been found in the form of dedications, yet most of them were in and around military bases, which housed, amongst others, Gallic Roman soldiers.[200] Similarly,

---

[191] Webster, *Celtic Religion in Roman Britain*, 41.

[192] Lewis, *Temples in Roman Britain*, 136.

[193] Miranda J. Green, *The Gods of Roman Britain* (Aylesbury, UK: Shire Publications, 1983), 37.

[194] Lewis, *Temples in Roman Britain*, 136. Meanwhile, the god Mercury had only three temples dedicated to him, the most well known at Uley, which are a source of several curse tablets.

[195] Hutchinson, *Bacchus in Roman Britain*, 109.

[196] Hutchinson, *Bacchus in Roman Britain*, 113-114.

[197] Joan P. Alcock, "The Concept of Genius in Roman Britain" in *Pagan Gods and Shrines of the Roman Empire*, ed. Martin Henig and Anthony King (Oxford: Oxford University Committee for Archaeology, 1986), 116ff.

[198] Lewis, *Temples in Roman Britain*, 136.

[199] Collingwood, *Roman Inscriptions of Britain* #1074, German goddess, from Lanchester.

[200] Catherine Johns, "Roman Bronze Stauette of Epona," *British Museum Quarterly* 36, no. 1/2 (1971), 37-39 and Aldhouse-Green, "Gallo-British Deities and their Shrines," 213.

Mercury/Lug did not appear to be nearly as popular in Britain as he was in Gaul.

The conflation of deities, or combining of the names and traits or gods from separate traditions, was a practical matter more than it was an attempt to create one religion out of many. Some of these combinations are very complex, as was true for the god Taranis, who was referred to in Lucan's *Pharsalia*.[201] His name was derived from the Celtic name for "thunderer."[202] Taranis became amalgamated with Jupiter because of the connected with thunder.[203] Taranis was a sky god, and horses and the solar wheel were iconography often associated with the sky in Celtic mythology.[204] So the images of this Romano-Celtic Jupiter, including versions found in Britain are an amalgam of iconography, including the Roman thunderbolt and human male form, along with Celtic icons such as the horse and solar wheel.[205] The conflation of deities was not always confined to the Celtic and Classical worlds, as in the case of the London hunter god, mentioned above.[206]

In some areas of Britain, native religious practices remained partially intact. Local Celtic deities persisted into the Roman era. In Godmanchester a triad of sky gods was worshiped and several depictions of them survive. There is no Classical equivalent to these gods, but a similar triad was recorded in Irish mythology.[207] While the number of depictions of Roman deities was higher than native deities in small towns, it was only slightly higher (51 Classical and 44 British) suggesting that the local, non-amalgamated gods were not quickly forgotten.[208] Other local traditions also survived. In parts of Huntingdonshire

---

[201] Lucan, *Pharsalia,* ed. C. E. Haskins (Hildesheim: G. Olms, 1971), I.444-446.

[202] Miranda J. Green, "Jupiter, Taranis and the Solar Wheel," in *Pagan Gods and Shrines of the Roman Empire,* ed. Martin Henig and Anthony King (Oxford: Oxford University Committee for Archaeology, 1986)Green, 65.

[203] Miranda Green, "Jupiter, Taranis and the Solar Wheel," 66.

[204] Miranda Green, "Jupiter, Taranis and the Solar Wheel," 69.

[205] Miranda Green, "Jupiter, Taranis and the Solar Wheel," 71-74.

[206] Ralph Merrifield, "The London Hunter-God," in *Pagan Gods and Shrines of the Roman Empire,* ed. Martin Henig and Anthony King (Oxford: Oxford University Committee for Archaeology, 1986), 91.

[207] H. J. M. Green, "Religious Cults at Roman Godmanchester," in *Pagan Gods and Shrines of the Roman Empire*, ed. Martin Henig and Anthony King (Oxford: Oxford University Committee for Archaeology, 1986), 42.

[208] Martin Millett, "Art in the 'Small Towns': 'Celtic' or 'Classical'?" in *Roman Life and Art in Britain: A Celebration in Honor of the Eighteenth Birthday of Jocelyn Toynbee,* vol. 2, ed. Julian Munby and Martin Henig (Oxford: British Archaeological Reports, 1977), 289.

particular thorn bushes had names and survived because of ancient taboos in their removal.[209]

Native Britons were not the only ones who embraced their deities; Romans praised them as well. One inscription from an ex-solider reads: "To the holy god Belatucadrus, Aurelius Tasulus, veteran, willingly and deservedly fulfills his vow."[210] In another inscription, Aelius Vibius, a centurion from the Twentieth Legion, fulfills his vow to the local god Antenociticus.[211] It is unclear how Roman came to worship these minor British deities, but they were not isolated incidents. Some Romans were so devoted to these British deities that they took them back to their homelands. The water spirit Coventina found along Hadrian's Wall at Carrawburgh was never twinned with a classical goddess, and the coins that were given to her in the fourth century show she was popular with the local military base for centuries.[212] Her popularity with some soldiers was such that her cult was exported, as two dedications to her were found in Southern Gaul and North-Western Spain.[213]

Native Britons had not given names to many of the divine forces they perceived in nature.[214] This is evident by the reoccurrence of Roman epitaphs without a corresponding native name in Romano-British contexts. These supposedly Roman gods were given attributes not known in the classical world. The attributes were characteristically Celtic. A good example is Silvanus. While this is a minor Roman deity, no less than three temples were dedicated to him in Britain. All three were in rural areas, the only areas still dominated by local British culture.[215] Depictions of Silvanus in Roman Britain are rarely of the deity in human form, as the classical aesthetic demands. Instead, the stag, Silvanus' pre-Roman icon, is found at holy sites.[216]

The ability of Romans to name the Britons' gods is remarkable. The Britons' acceptance of these Roman names is even more extraordinary. Superficially this may appear to be a show of power by the Romans, their attempt to prove their superior civilization by proclaiming their ability to name the gods of other cultures. However it is far more likely that the Romans named the deities of

---

[209] H. J. M. Green, "Religious Cults at Roman Godmanchester," 50.

[210] Collingwood, *Roman Inscriptions of Britain* I #887.

[211] Collingwood, *Roman Inscriptions of Britain* I #1327

[212] Aldhouse-Green, "Gallo-British Deities and their Shrines," 206.

[213] Aldhouse-Green, "Gallo-British Deities and their Shrines," 207.

[214] Green, "Religious Cults at Roman Godmanchester," 39

[215] Lewis, *Temples in Roman Britain*, 136.

[216] Green, *The Gods of Roman Britain*, 37.

Britons, while amalgamating other deities with their own, because it helped the Romans cope with a world they did not understand.

Another amalgamation was the goddesses Sulis and Minerva. The temple of Sulis-Minerva at Bath is one of the most studied Romano-British temples; it is also the site of the huge cache of curse tablets that will be reviewed in the next two chapters. The question is, is it typical example of Romano-British religion, or is it in some way abnormal. If it is a poor example of Roman and British fusion, if it is primarily British or Roman, Bath cache cannot be used to demonstrate Romano-British beliefs. When analyzed, the tablets, temple, and surrounding area are all typically Romano-British. The temple of Sulis-Minerva is a perfect example of how two different traditions found common ground and created a whole new tradition, the Romano-British religious tradition.

As the springs were the domain of Sulis-Minerva, who had the power to grant certain favors, the tablets were predominantly addressed to her and request favors she was known to perform. A quick review of the tablets confirms this, as most are directed to her and ask for justice or vengeance. Since the majority of the British curse tablets were found in Bath, incorporating them into the statistical data gives the impression that pleas to Sulis-Minerva for justice were the primary utilization of curse tablets in Britain. While there is a possibility of skewed statistics with the incorporation of the Bath tablets into the data set, is it is not necessarily the case. Many springs and graves, as of yet unexcavated, may hold a plethora of curse tablets, but it is also possible, although unlikely, that Bath was the only major site of curse tablets deposited in Britain.

In determining how representative the Bath and the Bath curse tablets were, it is necessarily to determine if the population of the city was representative of Britain. Before the Roman conquest, there was no permanent settlement at Bath. [217] However, there is evidence that the Britons viewed the spring at Bath as sacred. Excavations have revealed that at least eighteen Celtic coins were thrown into, or fell into, the spring.[218] There was also a causeway and gravel found in pre-Roman layers around the spring.[219] While this is admittedly meager evidence of any sort of worship of the spring, the location's geology must be taken into account. Due to its proximity to an oft-flooding stream, the size and shape of the

---

[217] Barry Cunliffe, *The City of Bath* (Gloucester: Alan Sutton, 1986), 14-15.

[218] Lyn Sellwood, "The Celtic Coins" in *The Temple of Sulis Minverva at* Bath, vol. 2: The *Finds from the Sacred Spring*, ed. Barry Cunnliffe (Oxford: Oxford University Committee for Archeology, 1988), 280.

[219] Aldhouse-Green, "Gallo-British Deities and their Shrines," 200.

spring changed over time. It is only when the Romans built walls around the spring that its shape was fixed. During the time that it was prone to flooding, items were churned up and a chronology is not possible.[220] Without a clear timeline of the artifacts found within the spring, it is not possible to say with assurance that the spring was of significant prehistoric religious importance. However, the rapid development of a semi-indigenous cult upon the arrival of the Romans suggests that the spring held a place of honor for the Britons.

During the reign of Claudius, Bath and the nearby areas began to be permanently populated. There may have been a fort nearby, which would have certainly brought attention to the spring.[221] The area around the spring became occupied in Claudian or Neronian eras.[222] Not long after, in the 60s or 70s C.E. the temple and baths were built.[223] The area was clearly built up by either Romans or Romanized Britons, judging by the architecture and archeological remains. The heart of the city, both spiritually and economically, was the springs and the temple that soon enclosed it.[224] The amount of coins shows how popular the spring was. Over 12,000 coins have been discovered in the spring, including four gold coins worth about two month's salary for a high-ranking Roman official.[225]

The Temple of Sulis Minerva presents some problems, which make it difficult to comprehend who came to the site and who would have deposited curse tablets in the spring. There is a debate as to who built the temple complex, Romans or natives.[226] Some scholars argue that since it was constructed shortly after the conquest proves that the temple "must represent a deliberate and official act of Romanization."[227] Also, the surviving parts of the altar portray Olympic deities in a classical aesthetic.[228] While Bath lies in an area of Britain that was not heavily Romanized before the invasion, it would not be out of the

---

[220] Cunliffe, *The City of Bath*, 14-15.

[221] Cunliffe, "The Sanctuary of Sulis Minerva at Bath," 1.

[222] Cunliffe, "The Sanctuary of Sulis Minerva at Bath," 1.

[223] Cunliffe, "The Sanctuary of Sulis Minerva at Bath," 1.

[224] J. Patrick Greene, "Bath and Other Small Western Towns," in *The 'Small Towns' of Roman Britain: Papers Presented to Conference, Oxford 1975*, ed. Warwick Rodwell and Trevor Rowley (Oxford: British Archaeological Reports, 1975), 133.

[225] Barry Cunliffe, *Roman Bath Discovered* (London: Routledge and Kegan Paul, 1984), 77 and Louise Revell, *Roman Imperialism and Local Identities* (Cambridge: Cambridge University Press, 2009), 122.

[226] Revell, *Roman Imperialism and Local Identities*, 118-119.

[227] Cunliffe, "The Sanctuary of Sulis Minerva at Bath," 2.

[228] Revell, *Roman Imperialism and Local Identities*, 120.

question to suggest that local Britons (or even Britons from further south) constructed the temple as a highly visible sign that they were Romanized. The temple was mostly likely a joint venture, conceived of interaction between prominent locals who wished to ingratiate themselves into the Roman political world and Romans who wished to find a common ground with their new subjects. Later inscriptions within the temple showed six military men and two men from other towns as some of the sixteen known patrons.[229] Clearly, the temple had wide appeal, and while Romans and Romanized Britons certainly made up the majority of the temple's visitors, its patrons were diverse.

The temple was dedicated to Sulis Minerva, although the twining of these two goddesses had no clear rational. Sulis was the personification of the spring and her powers before the conquest are unclear.[230] Some scholars speculate that "the shrine was endowed with healing properties."[231] Yet the characteristic ex-votos, tiny metal reproductions of the body part healed, are not present.[232] Although the spring at Bath had a reputation to heal later in history, it appears that this was not the case when the spring was in the guise of Sulis. It appears that Sulis was not a healing goddess, and her powers were only alluded to in one other way, the curse tablets themselves. Although not all the tablets explain what is being asked of the deity, many do. In all but three of the curse tablets, the supplicant is asking the goddess to return a stolen item and punish the thief. The other three tablets are similarly asking for vengeance. All but three are addressed to Minerva, Sulis, or a combination of the two. This suggests that Sulis and the amalgamated Sulis Minerva were conceived as being goddesses of justice.

The example of the Sulis-Minerva and her temple in Bath illustrate how Romans and Britons found common ground in their religions and combine their similar aspects. Outside the Roman cities and army bases, Roman religion could not survive untouched by Celtic tradition, and the most popular gods and cults incorporated popular deities and practices from Britain and abroad. Some superficial changes occurred, such as the building of permanent temples, but the basic British religion was not damaged by the Roman conquest, it was merely enhanced by new gods and practices.

---

[229] Revell, *Roman Imperialism and Local Identities*, 129.

[230] Aldhouse-Green, "Gallo-British Deities and their Shrines," 205.

[231] Cunliffe, "The Sanctuary of Sulis Minerva at Bath," 10.

[232] Revell, *Roman Imperialism and Local Identities*, 122.

Chapter 4: The Spiritual World of the Romano-Britons

I curse Tretia Maria and her life and mind and memory and liver and lungs mixed up together, and her words, thoughts and memory; thus may she be unable to speak what things are concealed, nor be able . . .[233]

The curse tablets that have been discovered in Britain can greatly improve our understanding of how Rome influenced the spiritual life of the British inhabitants. The deviations of curse tablet style in Britain illustrate what was important to the Romano-Britons and how they adapted classical culture to fit with their own concepts of the how the universe worked. Whereas the author who cursed Tretia Maria used a traditional Greco-Roman curse, with the word "I curse" and a list of body parts to be bound, the majority of curse tablet writers in Roman Britain deviated from the classical norms. The insights garnered from the curse tablets, together with other data about the religious and spiritual life of Roman Britain show that the Britons were adaptable, yet unwilling to give up their unique spiritual beliefs.

The British curse tablets give an interesting, albeit limited, insight into the spiritual world of the Romano-Britons. Around 150 curse tablets have been deciphered, with several more that have been discovered but remain in a rolled up state. More than half were discovered in the springs at Bath, but around sixty have been discovered from around the province in dozens of sites, proving that the practice of creating curse tablets had been popular in Britain. Some of the curse tablets are only remnants, revealing just a word or name. Few have been found completely intact, but much can be gleaned from the *defixiones* about how the Britons adapted Roman practices and merged them with native beliefs.

Curse tablets, as a form of magic, was frowned upon by Roman society.[234] The Britons and Romans did not have the same definition of magic, since magic was a social construct. There is no evidence that the British had a concept of "magic," because there was no strict definition of religion in the society to oppose it to.[235] Taboos were the closest approximation to magic for the British.

---

[233] Collingwood, *The Roman Inscriptions of Britain*, 7; Appendix I #88.

[234] Curse tablets in the Roman world constituted a "liminal phenomena" which was not considered a part of society and thus shunned. Britons, however, were able to integrate them with their society. Victor W. Turner, *The Ritual Process: Structure and Anti-Structure* (Chicago: Aldine Publishing Company, 1969), 96.

[235] Fritz Graf, "Excluding the Charming: The Development of the Greek Concept of Magic," in *Ancient Magic and Ritual Power*, ed. Marvin Meyer and Paul Mirecki (Boston: Brill Academic

Druids supposedly used divination, but other activities that are considered magic did not appear to be a part of British culture.[236] Roman concepts of magic only arrived with the Romans themselves. Romans introduced the Britons to various new rituals and traditions, including the creation of curse tablets and the wearing of charms.[237]

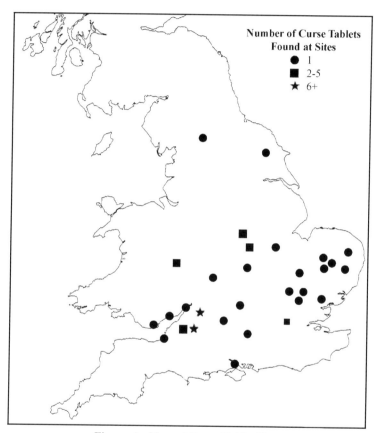

Figure 4 - Map of Curse Tablet Sites

The curse tablets can help illuminate which deities were important to the Romano-Britons, and what they believed the gods could be compelled to do. It is not clear whether a god's popularity or its perceived powers was the deciding factor in choosing a deity to address in a curse tablet. A god's powers, including

Publishers, 2001), 40.

[236] Cicero, *De Deivinatione*, I.41

[237] A good example of this is the tradition Greco-Roman charm in R. S. O. Tomlin, "A Bilingual Roman Charm for Health and Victory," *Zeitschrift für Papyrologie und Epigraphick* 149 (2004): 256.

its ability to implement a curse tablet would have been culturally dictated. Initially, Britons would not of had a firm grasp on the powers that Roman or a Celtic/Roman hybrid deities had, but would be more inclined to assume that they held the power to fulfill curse tablets. They also would have deferred to Romans in their choice of gods, and employ similar deities in the creation of curse tablets. And a Roman from Veii would have as much faith in Mercury in performing a curse in Britain as he would in Italy. However, local custom may have changed the options of the incoming Britons about the powers of the gods. After all, native British religious custom had influenced the Romans in other ways.

When the names of deities were given in the curse tablets, the names of the gods invoked to carry out the curse tablets were a mixture of Roman and Celtic deities. Understandably most (19 or 86%) of the Bath tablets were addressed to Sulis, Minerva or Sulis-Minerva. There were also Bath tablets dedicated to Mercury and Mars (one to Mercury, two to Mars). Mercury was especially popular for curse tablet dedications, with eleven overall, and the temple of Mercury in Uley was the site of several *defixiones* discoveries. One of these tablets was addressed to Mars-Mercury, but the rest simply used the name Mercury, showing how the Gallic tradition of paring Mercury with local deities, especially Lug, did not occur widely in Britain. Two tablets addressed to Mars (one as Mars-Silvanus) were found outside of Bath, at Marlborough Downs and Uley.[238] This is not too surprising since Mercury and Mars were popular in both Britain and elsewhere in the Empire. The four tablets addressed to Neptune are somewhat strange, since Neptune did not appear to have a large local following. The location of the tablets, found in Brandon, Caistor St. Edmund, Hamble Estuary, and London, were all riverbeds, and three of the tablets allude to significant thefts.[239] This suggests that these tablets were written either by wealthy Romano-Britons or their location inspired them to write to the god of the sea.

Several deities were only mentioned once in the curse tablets: Minerva, Jupiter, Nodens, Niskus, Virtue, Deana, Nemesis, Mars-Mercury, 'Womb,' and Maglus. The invocation of the Roman gods Jupiter, Virtue, Minerva, Mars-Mercury and Nemesis are all understandable, as they are deities concerned with justice. It is unclear if Deana is a misspelling of Diana or a local deity, but since the subject of the curse tablet was armor, it seems likely that the hunter goddess would be invoked.[240] Three purely Celtic deities were addressed, which shows

---

[238] Appendix I #94 and #107

[239] Appendix I #73, #75, #81, and #92.

that the practice of making curse tablets was not confined to completely Romanized Britons. The tablet to Celtic god Nodens was found in Lydney Park, where the god's temple lay.[241] Niskus and Maglus were both Celtic deities, but nothing is known about either of them, these tablets are the only recorded instance of their names.[242] There is nothing startling about the gods that were invoked, as the Roman deities are ones that were routinely called upon and the addition of the Celtic deities reflects the diverse background of the Romano-Britons.

Table 1 - Deities Invoked in the Curse Tablets

	From Bath	From Outside of Bath	Total
Sulis	12 54%	0 0%	12 23%
Sulis-Minerva	6 27%	0 0%	6 11%
Minerva	1 5%	0 0%	1 2%
Mercury	1 5%	10 33%	11 21%
Mars	2 9%	2 7%	4 8%
Neptune	0 0%	4 13%	4 8%
God	0 0%	3 10%	3 6%
Other	0 0%	8 26%	8 15%

The Christian God is referred to three or four times. However, two of these examples are not traditional curse tablets. The golden scrolls from Oxford and Billingsford both obey the rules for curse tablets, yet they are in Greek and protect instead of harm. The Oxford scroll was for the protection of an unborn child, while the Billingsford scroll was for health and victory.[243] The Billingsford example is particularly interesting, stating "Iao, Abrasax . . . alblanathanalba, give health and victory to Tiberius Claudius Similis whom Herennia Marcellina

[240] Appendix I #91.

[241] Appendix I #93.

[242] Appendix I #81 and #84.

[243] Appendix I #97 and #71.

bore." The name Iao, or ιαω, was a Greek form of Yahweh that was often associated with Gnosticism. Since both of these are both in Greek and show remarkable knowledge of Eastern magical formulae, neither of these was made by a Romano-Briton. A curse tablet that was created by a native Briton that addressed God was found in Eccles Villa and dates from the fourth century C.E.[244] The tablet, which contains the rare Celtic name Butu, apparently involves theft, the most common reason for Romano-British curse tablets. There is also an incomplete tablet that begged "your Majesty" which could have been referring to God.[245] The few references to God show that curse tablets were still being employed after people converted in Britain, which was similar to other parts of the Empire. But like elsewhere in the Empire, the curse tablets did not continue on after the fall of the Empire.

The small number of Christian curse tablets is due to the slow spread of Christianity in Britain, not because of any taboos against magic within Christianity. Christianity appeared in Britain in the late second or early third century. However, it was not until the mid-fourth century, after Imperial promotion of the religion, that it began to gain a large following in Britain.[246] Few churches were built in Britain before 330.[247] In the fourth century, the building of pagan temples slowed considerably, and only one temple, in the country, was built in the fifth century.[248] While there were dozen of churches built in Roman Britain, there did not appear to be widespread adherence to Catholic Christianity. Pagan sacrifices of animals were found in a London church from the era of Rome's abandonment of Britain.[249]

The subject matter of the Romano-British curse tablets is the most intriguing dimension of the *defixiones*. Curse tablets demanding justice are relatively rare outside Britain, but the seventy four tablets justice tablets dominate the British catalogue, accounting for 53% of the total tablets. Outside of Britain, Tomlin counts just twenty theft tablets, only six of which were in Latin.[250] Tablets that appeal for justice were similar to the theft tablets and they account for 6% of the

---

[244] Appendix I #79.

[245] Appendix I #124.

[246] Dorothy Watts, Religion in Late Roman Britain: Forces of Change (London: Routledge, 1998), 2.

[247] Watts, *Religion in Late Roman Britain*, 13.

[248] Lewis, *Temples in Roman Britain*, 139.

[249] Merrifield, "The London Hunter-God," 85.

[250] R. S. O. Tomlin, "The Curse Tablets" in *The Temple of Sulis Minverva at Bath, vol. 2, The Finds from the Sacred Spring*, ed. Barry Cunnliffe (Oxford: Oxford University Committee for Archeology, 1988), 61-62.

tablets. Four of these are from Bath, including a typical tablet that curses any of the six people who lied under oath in the Temple of Sulis.[251] While the worship of Sulis-Minerva as a goddess of justice would explain the Bath tablets, the overwhelming number of other theft and justice tablets remains unexplained. Even without the Bath tablets, the British justice tablets account for the majority of Latin justice tablets. There are several factors that may have been at work to create this abnormality. The stolen items, when named, tended to be high-value items, such as cloaks, rings, and even draft animals, attesting to the wealth of some of the Romano-Britons. It suggests that there might have been a higher rate of crime than in other provinces, or a lower rate in capturing thieves and putting them on trial. Either of these two factors would have made it necessary to ask for supernatural help in retrieving goods. The beliefs of the native Britons may have influenced the creation of justice tablets. The Britons may have believed that the gods should not have been invoked in curse tablets unless it was for matters of justice instead of personal gain. Theft will be explored in greater detail in Chapter 5.

Table 2: Reason For Curse Tablet

	From Bath	From Outside of Bath	Total
Theft	36 52%	30 53%	66 53%
Vengeance / Justice	4 6%	4 7%	8 6%
Other	2 3%	2 3%	4 3%
Unknown	26 38%	21 37%	47 38%

Many of the curse tablets found in Britain only give hints as to the purpose behind the *defixiones*. Two of these can be read to insinuate rationale other than theft. The first is from Caerleon and it asks Nemesis to curse anyone who wears a pair of boots and cloak.[252] Ferguson suggests that this was sabotage by a cavalry regiment or chariot team against a rival.[253] If the Caerleon tablet is concerned with chariot racing, it would be in good company. Chariot racing

---

[251] Tomlin, "The Curse Tablets," 226.

[252] Collingwood, *Roman Inscriptions of Britain* I, #323.

[253] John Ferguson, *The Religions of the Roman Empire* (Ithaca, NY: Cornell University Press, 1970), 166.

tablets are common around the Empire. One found in Rome is quite extensive in the names cursed.[254] Another found in the circus of Antioch is even more thorough, a full sixty-one lines.[255] However, there is little other evidence of chariot racing in Britain, so the tablet may refer to Ferguson's other suggestion, rival cavalry regiments, or to some other sport. Curse tablets concerning sports other than chariot racing have been uncovered, such as the one against several runners in Corinth.[256] It may also be that this was a poorly worded justice tablet.

The other non-justice curse tablet is from Old Harlow and reads: "To the god Mercury, I entrust to you my affair with Eterna and her own self, and may Timotheus feel no jealousy of me at the risk of his life-blood."[257] This could indicate a love affair, but Webster suggests the tablet results from business dealing between Eterna and the writer of the curse tablet.[258] Hundreds of love and business related curse tablets have been unearthed from around the Empire. Business tablets were most commonly placed underneath the place of business and refer to the business or occupation of the target, such as the curse against the blacksmiths placed under a smithy in Athens.[259] However, this tablet was located in a well, which was the most common location to find a tablet in Britain, but it does not shed light on the tablet's purpose.[260] Love tablets almost always used the verb "I bind" in their construction and mention copious numbers of body parts. The Old Harlow tablet does not appear to conform to either of conventions, so it is unclear what the purpose of the tablet was.

The placement of the curse tablets in water, in Bath and around Britain, harkens back to an ancient British tradition. It appears that placing curse tablets in water was just the continuation of that tradition.[261] Celtic beliefs held that springs and rivers were often sacred, and they were the focus of many rituals and practices.[262] The offerings placed in the water for the gods and spirits are among the most beautiful and impressive items that have been found in Britain.

---

[254] Jordon, "A Curse on Charioteers," 141.

[255] Hollman, "A Curse Tablet from the Circus at Antioch," 61.

[256] David Jordon, "Inscribed Lead Tablets from the Games in the Sanctuary of Poseidon," *Hesperia* 63, no. 1 (1994): 116-118.

[257] Wacher, *Roman Britain,* 240.

[258] Webster, *Celtic Religion in Roman Britain,* 136.

[259] Jamie B. Cubera and David R. Jordan, "A Curse Tablet from the 'Industrial District' Near the Athenian Agora," *Hesperia* 67, no. 2 (1998): 215 and 217.

[260] For full information, see Appendix 1 #96

[261] Alcock, *Daily Life of the Pagan Celts,* 137.

[262] Ross, *Pagan Celtic Britain,* 20, 22-30.

The Waterloo Bridge helmet, Battersea shield, and Wandsworth shield bosses were all purposely placed in the water.[263] From the Bronze Age onwards, swords, spears, helmets, shields, and other warrior paraphernalia were placed in the sacred waters.[264] While the practice of depositing metalwork in water was still a part of British culture when the Romans invaded, it had decreased from the early Iron Age.[265]

Neither the items deposited in the water nor the location of the deposits was incidental. Most of the items deposited were made especially to be given to the water deities. Few of the weapons or armor had ever been used. Many bronze weapons and tools were found in the Eastern Fenland, specifically at the end of long wooden causeways that led to the edge of the deeper waters.[266] Although the area of water was large, only one part of these fens was considered sacred. The offerings were often found in water far from where they were created, and the water locations are out of the way themselves, such as Dainton in Devon and Jarelshof in the Shetlands.[267] Due to the expense of these gifts, it seems likely that the upper classes of Britons left these offerings to the spirits of water for themselves and for their communities. It was the duty of the elites to give these sacrifices and their honor would have been greatly diminished had they not performed their civic obligations. [268] Items that have been excavated from the later Iron Age in sacred waters were of a worn, often broken, condition, indicating only a passing interest in devoting goods to the gods of the water.[269] Deposits of valuable goods into water all but disappeared upon the arrival of the Romans.

Much like the Britons, the Romans had numerous water deities and viewed most water as some way sacred, which was why the Romans often placed *defixiones* in the water.[270] Small offerings, usually in the form of coins, have been found in springs and wells all over Roman Britain. In the excavations at Portchester castle alone, ten Roman bronze coins were found in the wells.[271]

---

[263] Barry Cunliffe, *Rome and the Barbarians* (New York: Henry Z Walck Inc, 1975), 89.

[264] Jean Louis Brunaux, *The Celtic Gauls: Gods, Rites and Sanctuaries*, trans. Daphne Nash (London: Seaby, 1988), 94.

[265] Barry Cunliffe, *Wessex to AD 1000* (London: Longman, 1993), 198.

[266] Michael Parker Pearson, *English Heritage Book of Bronze Age Britain* (London: B. T. Batsford, 1993), 113.

[267] Pearson, *English Heritage Book of Bronze Age Britain*, 116.

[268] Pearson, *English Heritage Book of Bronze Age Britain*, 117.

[269] De la Bèdoyère, *Roman Britain*, 251.

[270] Cunliffe, *Rome and the Barbarians*, 89.

Some springs, especially thermal springs, were thought to have the power to heal. Roman healing springs are often recognized by the votive offerings found nearby. They are small scale representations of the body part(s) that a person wanted healed, or the god had healed. The sacred healing spring of Les Roches in Gaul was the site of one such cache.[272]

Table 3: Location of Curse Tablets

	From Bath	Outside of Bath	Total
In Water	69 100%	6 11%	75 60%
In Temples	0 0%	16 29%	16 13%
Under Buildings	0 0%	11 20%	11 9%
In Cemeteries	0 0%	1 2%	1 1%
Other Locations	0 0%	8 14%	8 6%
Unknown	0 0%	11 20%	11 9%

Since both Roman and British societies placed such importance on springs, it is natural that the Bath spring was the locus of religious and spiritual activity. Yet the Bath cache of *defixiones* can be deceiving, giving the impression that all British curse tablets were placed in water. Besides the Bath tablets, few (6, or 11%) were placed in wells or springs. There were many wells scattered around Britain in which to place a tablet, since most towns in Britain had wells instead of the typical Roman aqueducts.[273] While wells did not have as much religious meaning as springs, they still proved to be the focus of some devotional activities. Caches of curse tablets have been found in other wells and springs in the Empire. Over sixty lead tablets have been found in a well in Caesarea Maritima in modern Israel.[274] One hundred have been found in the wells of the agora at Athens.[275]

---

[271] Barry Cunliffe, *Excavations at Portchester Castle Vol. 2: Saxon* (London: The Society of Antiquaries of London, 1976), 67, 69, and 88-90.

[272] Cunliffe, *Rome and the Barbarians*, 97.

[273] Allason-Jones, *Daily Life in Roman Britain*, 64-65.

[274] Barbara Burrell, "'Curse Tablets' from Caesarea," *Near Eastern Archeology* 61, no. 2 (1998): 128.

The lack of any other caches of curse tablets from these wells is puzzling, but there are a few possible explanations. Archeologists have concentrated their energies on excavating large public structures and military instillations, and therefore may have yet to discover more caches. Wells used in Roman Britain often remained in use for centuries afterwards, creating layers of debris that are difficult to sift through. From thoroughly excavated wells such as the ones at Portchester Castle it is clear that there was reverence paid to the spirits of the water.[276] It may have been that only a few water spirits and gods, such as Sulis, were able to perform the magic needed in the curse tablets.

Outside of Britain, most curse tablets were found in graves, primarily in graves of the prematurely deceased.[277] It was easy to find the graves of the prematurely dead. Many, if not most, gravestones gave the age of death of the interred. Most followed the pattern of: "To the memory of . . . aged __ years."[278] Even babies and children had gravestones, such as the one that was put up by Lucius Semprobianus for his two year old son.[279] Perhaps the most surprising thing about the location of the British curse tablets was that very few were found in cemeteries. Part of this may have to do with the British practices concerning death and their deviation from the Mediterranean standard.

The techniques used by the ancient Britons in their disposal of the dead changed significantly during the millennia before the Roman conquest, making it difficult to ascertain how the Roman occupation changed their burial habits. Burial customs varied not only by period but by location. For example, in Silchester cremation, ashes and bones buried in a butt-beaker was custom.[280] In Wessex the cremation of the body and its subsequent placement in a cemetery was the preferred method of burial by the end of the second millennium B.C.E., but a less organized form of burial occurred during the middle of the first millennium B.C.E.[281] Similarly, in Kent, formal burials disappear around 1000

---

[275] David Jordan, "Defixiones from a Well Near the Southwest Corner of the Athenian Agora," *Hesperia* 54, no. 3 (1985): 205.

[276] Cunliffe, *Excavations at Portchester Castle*, vol. 2, 67, 69, and 88-90.

[277] D'Ambra, "Racing with Death," 348.

[278] V. E. and A. H. Nash-Williams, *Catalogue of the Roman Inscribes and Sculpted Stones Found at Caerleon, Monmouthshire* (Cardiff: National Museum of Wales and Press Board of the University of Wales, 1935), 34-35.

[279] F. Haverfield, *Catalogue of the Roman Inscribed and Sculptured Stones in the Grosvenor Museum, Chester* (Chester: Chester and North Wales Archaeological Society, 1900), 51.

[280] George C. Boon, *Roman Silchester: The Archaeology of a Romano-British Town* (London: Max Parrish, 1957), 132.

B.C.E. but start to reappear around 300 C.E.[282] The disappearance of formal cremation and burials in the early to mid first century is unexplained, however the actual funeral pyre appeared to always have had a greater significance than the burial, so it is not necessarily a reversal of beliefs or values.[283] They only strata of British society that seemed concerned with burials were the upper classes. The number and quality of grave goods were indicators of status.[284] The elites of Roman society were similarly buried with amphorae of wine, pottery, and native metalwork.[285]

The Britons had a much looser concept of death rituals than the Romans, yet with the Roman conquest, British burials became increasingly uniform, which makes the lack of graveside curse tablets more confusing. Grave goods were common in Roman Britain, just as they were in the rest of the Empire. Many consisted of simple goods, such as glass phials and pottery.[286] Many shoes have been found in Romano-British graves, either because the deceased required them for eternity, or because they were not put on the body prior to its cremation/burial.[287] A cremation found in Sompting dating from the Severian era is typical of Romano-British burials. The remains were placed in a jar, along with other dishes and a coin for Charon, all of which appeared to have been buried in a wooden box together.[288] In the latter half of the fourth century C.E. there was a decline in grave goods, and therefore possibly a change in the beliefs about the afterlife.[289] Many tombs were marked by gravestones, which provided simple information the lives of common Romano-Britons. Names, military ranks, and age of death are all commonly inscribed on tombstones.

Only one curse tablet was found in a Roman cemetery. The Clothall curse

---

[281] Cunliffe, *Wessex to AD 1000*, 195, 231.

[282] Timothy Champion, "Prehistoric Kent," in *The Archaeology of Kent to AD 800*, ed. John H Williams (Woodbridge, UK: Boydell Press and Kent County Council, 2007), 111 and 115.

[283] Rosalind Niblett, "The Native Elite and their Funerary Practices from the First Century BC to Nero," in *A Companion to Roman Britain*, ed. Malcolm Todd (Malden, MA: Blackwell Publishing, 2004), 34.

[284] Cunliffe, *Wessex to 1000 AD*, 231.

[285] Niblett, "The Native Elite and their Funerary Practices from the First Century BC to Nero," 31.

[286] Wright, *Uriconium: A Historical Account of the Ancient Roman City and of the Excavations Made Upon its Site at Wroxeter in Shropshire* (London: Longmans, Green, & Co., 1872), 355.

[287] J. L. MacDonald, "Religion," in *The Roman Cemetery at Lankhills*, ed. Giles Clarke (Oxford: Clarendon Press, 1979), 407.

[288] C. J. Ainsworth and H. B. A. Ratcliffe-Densham, "Spectroscopy and a Roman Cremation from Sompting, Sussex," *Britannia* 5 (1974): 310.

[289] MacDonald, "Religion," 423-433.

tablet, which was found in 1930, was discovered amongst the urns of a Romano-British cemetery.[290] This tablet was the most traditional of any of the curse tablets found in Britain. Not only was it in a grave, but it was pierced with five nails and it was vindictive, cursing someone to be "labeled old like putrid gore." The excavations of other cemeteries have not uncovered any other buried curse tablets. Many Romano-British cemeteries have been found and excavated, but amongst the thousands of graves, only Clothall has given up a *defixiones*.[291] Pieces of lead have been routinely found in graves, but they almost certainly are pieces of decayed coffin linings.[292]

The unusual absence of curse tablets in Roman Britain appears to be related to the subject matter of the Romano-British curse tablets. Very few of the tablets are as vengeful as the Clothall curse, noted above.[293] The majority (66 or 52%) ask for justice or the return of stolen goods.[294] In order to accomplish this, the goods are given to the god, who will punish the thieves. Putting a curse tablet in a grave to retrieve goods would not work. Neither spirits nor the infernal deities are associated with the retrieval of stolen items.

Traditionally, the only curse tablets that were placed in or around temples were those concerned with theft. Many were placed outside the temple on holy ground, where the public, including the thief, could see the *defixiones*. Several of the tablets found in Roman Britain were found in or around a temple. Along with the Bath tablets, the dozens of tablets that were found at Uley, the second largest cache found in Britain, were located around temples.[295] All of the Uley tablets were found around the temple of Mercury, and all of the tablets found there that name a deity invoke Mercury.[296] Addressing the god of commerce and thieves was a natural choice when attempting to retrieve stolen or lost property. The tendency of the Romano-Britons to place *defixiones* relating to theft in temples was in keeping with the traditional Greco-Roman practices.

---

[290] Appendix I #77 and Collingwood, *Roman Inscriptions of Britain* I #221.

[291] One of the largest Roman Burial sites found in Britain, with almost 500 graves and no *defixiones* in MacDonald, "Religion," 404ff.

[292] Alan McWhirr, Linda Viner, and Calvin Wells, *Romano-British Cemeteries at Cirencester* (Cirencester: Cirencester Excavation Committee, 1982), microfiche 2-e03.

[293] Collingwood, *Roman Inscriptions of Britain* I #221. "*uetus / quodmodo sanies / significatur / Tacita deficta.*" The tablet is fully explored in Appendix I #77.

[294] See Appendix II, table 2.

[295] Many tablets have been found at the temple on West Hill in Uley, yet very few of them survived intact or have been unfolded/unrolled. The best preserved *defixiones* from Uley are in Appendix I #107-120.

[296] Appendix 1, #107-120.

Given the traditions of both the British and the Romans, the placement of theft related curse tablets into the spring of Sulis in Bath makes perfect sense. Not long after the Roman conquest, or possibly some time beforehand, Sulis was connected to justice. Her spring was a logical place to connect to her. When the Romans built a temple enclosing the spring, the location became doubly sacred. The enclosed spring would have been the ideal location to place a curse tablet demanding the return of a stolen item. That is way the majority of the curse tablets have been dated to the period when the spring was enclosed.[297] Both the British and Roman traditions were being embraced by placing *defixiones* into the enclosed spring.

Eleven curse tablets (9% of the total) have been found under buildings other than temples.[298] In many cases it is unclear if the buildings were built before or after the tablet was deposited, although it is safe to assume that that the tablet was placed under the building, since the buildings were often public ones where the victim of the curse could have visited. Elsewhere in the Empire, the majority of *defixiones* that were placed under dwellings were cursing businesses that were in that building, such as the Athenian curse tablet found under a smithy that cursed the smithies that worked there. [299] Few tablets recovered from under buildings in Britain give the motivation for the curse. Most were intended to inflict great harm upon a person, but no mention of theft or business is given. A typical example of such a tablet comes from under a Roman amphitheatre in Caerleon reads: "Lady Nemesis, I give thee a cloak and a pair of boots; let him who wore them not redeem them except with the life of his Blood-red charger."[300] This appears to be a theft tablet, like so many other British *defixiones*, and it was buried at this location because this was presumably the site of the theft.

Occasionally sacrifices were given to the gods or spirits when depositing a curse tablet in the Mediterranean world. Cats and dogs were common sacrifices as evidenced by the curse tablets themselves as well as remains found with the tablets. This practice does not seem to have found any devotees in Britain. The lack of sacrificed animals was not due to any abhorrence of killing dogs or cats in rituals. Sacrifices of dogs and cats have been found in Roman Britain in non-curse tablet related rituals.[301] Culturally, the native Britons rarely made

---

[297] Revell, *Roman Imperialism and Local Identities*, 124.

[298] See Appendix II, table 3 for more information.

[299] Cubera, "A Curse Tablet from the 'Industrial District' Near the Athenian Agora," 215, 217.

[300] Appendix I #74.

[301] Ralph Merrifield, *Roman London* (London: Cassell, 1969), 67-68 and Merrifield, "The London Hunter-God," 85.

sacrifices, except in extreme cases. The Romans, on the other hand, had a long history of performing sacrifices on a regular basis. Most sacrifices in Roman Britain occurred in Classical temples and used traditional Roman victims. Sheep and goats were the most common animals sacrificed.[302] Temples that were located on British sacred springs, such as Bath and Lydney, show little evidence of animal sacrifice, suggesting that local tradition trumped Roman tradition in these locations.[303] Votive offerings, however, were much the same in Britain as they were in the rest of the Empire. Coins, jewelry, and other small offerings deposited in shrines and temples, while sometimes Celtic in style, were Roman in their origin. The lack of sacrificed animals accompanying the tablets was probably due to the British tradition trumping the Roman tradition of sacrifices.

Table 4: Physical Traits, When Known, of the Curse Tablets

	From Bath	From Outside Bath	Total
Folded	24	19	43
	35%	34%	34%
Pierced	6	9	15
	9%	16%	12%
Made of Lead	7	52	59
	12%	93%	51%
Made of Tin/Lead Alloy	48	1	49
	81%	2%	43%
Made of Another Material	4	3	7
	7%	5%	6%

The original reason for using lead in curse tablets derived from lead's cold and common nature. It is unclear if the Britons understood the symbolism of the lead or if they had read the manuals from the Mediterranean that stated that lead was the correct material for curse tablets. From the cache of Bath tablets, it appears that the Britons were either unaware or uninterested as to how curse tablets were constructed elsewhere. Only 10% were lead, whereas 70% were alloys, usually tin and lead, the rest were of other or unknown materials. The practical reason for this was that the sheeting used in the city of Bath was an alloy and thus any scraps used for the tablets were also alloys. Either the patrons of the Temple of Sulis Minerva were less Romanized than other creators of curse tablets in Roman Britain or that there was a separate tradition that is unknown to

---

[302] King, "Animal Remains from Temples in Roman Britain," 333.

[303] King, "Animal Remains from Temples in Roman Britain," 363.

us that lessened the importance of lead in the creation of curse tablets addressed to Sulis Minerva. The reason for the use of alloy is not knowable, but apparently the writers of the curse tablets were not bothered by the fact that they were using a somewhat unorthodox material.

The surviving magic manuals often dictate that the piece of lead with the curse tablet upon it be folded several times before having nails driven through it. However, 67% of the British curse tablets are were either rolled up or left flat, not folded.[304] This may have to do with the fact that they were predominantly found in springs and wells. Springs and wells from outside of Britain have yielded numerous curse tablets, including many rolled tablets.[305] Perhaps it was thought that the tablet would be hidden and would never be read at the bottom of the well, whereas there was a chance that tablets left under buildings and in graves would be discovered and read. Yet this is not a wholly sufficient answer to the problem.

Driving nails through the folded curse tablet was the penultimate step in creating a curse tablet, and was meant to symbolize the pinning down of their victim's will. This was such a crucial step that the word *defixiones* derives from the action of pinning down the tablet with a nail, and by doing so, nailing down the fate of the victim. Fifteen of the British curse tablets had nails, but that means that 88% of the tablets were not pierced. Only six of the Bath tablets were nailed, although there are a couple of others that showed signs that they might have been nailed down. Nine tablets from outside Bath have also been found with a nail hole, but without any trace of nails.

While many pierced tablets preserve only the scar of being pierced, several were found with nails still embedded in them or with nails lying nearby. Iron nails were always used. Iron nails were the most commonly used nails in Roman Britain for everyday use as well as for sealing coffins.[306] Although they would have been easy to obtain, it appears that the Britons did not feel compelled to use nails in the creation of their curse tablets. Both the folding and the piercing of the tablets, nearly universal outside of Britain, was not a common practice. In the Mediterranean world these acts were symbolic, but the native Britons did not have these symbols in their cultural lexicon. Although they might have know

---

[304] See Appendix II for more details.

[305] Burrell, "'Curse Tablets' from Caesarea,"128.

[306] Leslie P. Wenham, *The Romano-British Cemetery at Trentholme Drive, York* (London: Her Majesty's Stationary Office, 1968), 39; Kelly Powell, "The Nails" in *Life and Death in a Roman City: Excavation of a Roman Cemetery with a Mass Grave at 120-122 London Road, Gloucester*, ed. Andrew Simmonds, Nicholas Marquez-Grant and Louis Loe (Oxford: Oxford Archeological Monograph No. 6, 2008), 115; and Giles Clarke, *The Roman Cemetery at Lankhills* (Oxford: Clarendon Press, 1979), 332-333.

about the rest of the Empire created curse tablets, the folding and piercing appeared to have no purpose for them, so they often discarded these steps.

Many of the British tablets consist of only names. This is not uncommon for curse tablets, although by the first century C.E., tablets had increased in their complexity elsewhere in the Empire. The inscriptions in the longer tablets do not appear to be from known magic manuals such as the *PGM*, but the similarity between the many of the Bath tablets suggests that there was either a manual known to the Britons or that the knowledge was passed along orally in the community. Several of the intact tablets concerning theft from Bath follow a similar pattern as this:

> *Docilianus son of Brucerus to the most holy goddess Sulis. I curse him who has stolen my hooded cloak, whether man or woman, slave or free, that . . . the goddess Sulis inflicts death upon . . . not allow him sleep or children now and in the future, until he has brought my cloak to the temple of her divinity.*[307]

There are many variations of this formula, such as tablets that include "whether boy or girl" and "whether pagan or Christian."[308]

Jeremy Burgess, in his thesis, "Formulaic Constructions in Curse Tablets from Roman Britain," counted four separate formula phrases from Roman Britain, although some tablets employed multiple formulas.[309] The tablet above contains both the "whether man or woman" and "do not permit" phrases. The other two were "I give to you" and "his own blood."[310] For whatever reason, tablets that contained the "do not permit" formula were common in Bath, but not anywhere else. This suggests that this formula was given to the curse tablet writers by temple priests or it was common knowledge in the town of Bath.

There is no evidence that professional magicians or priests wrote the curse tablets for patrons. In the Greek East caches have been discovered where several of the *defixiones* were written in the same hand, suggesting that they were written by a professional on behalf of patrons. Yet in the Bath cache, only two tablets appear to be in the same hand.[311] Some tablets were probably dictated by

---

[307] Originally: " *Docilianus / Bruceri [filius] / deae sanctissim[a]e / Suli / devoveo eum [q]ui / caracellam mean / involaverit si / vir si femina si / servus si liber / ut . . . us dea Sulis / maximo letum / [a]digat nec ei so/mnum permit*" Reverse/continued "*tat nec natos nec / nascentes do/[ne]c caracallam / meam ad tem/plum sui numi/nus per[t]ulerit*" See Appendix I #8 for full details.

[308] i.e. Appendix I #19 and #4.

[309] Jeremy Burgess, "Formulaic Constructions in Curse Tablets from Roman Britain," (MA thesis, University of Hawaii at Manoa, 2002), 52.

[310] Appendix I #47 and #25.

someone who was not literate, and others were probably written with the assistance of temple priests, but there does not appear to be a curse writing business in Britain. This should have made the tablets less formulaic and more personal, since there was no one dictating how the tablet should be written. Yet the form of the Romano-British tablets showed little deviation from each other. Although they were formulaic, these curse tablets were not as legalistic as curse tablets from elsewhere in the Empire.[312]

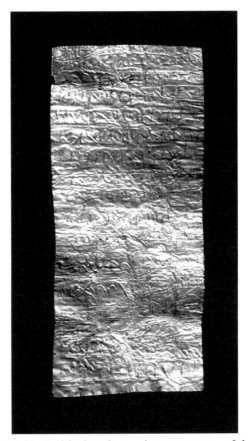

Figure 5 - Golden "Tablet" with charakteres, image courtesy of the British Museum.

The lack of *voces mysticae* and *charakteres* in the curse tablets is startling. There are several instances where it is unclear if words were poorly written or if they were intended to be *voces mysticae*, magic words. In most cases it appears to

---

[311] Revell, *Roman Imperialism and Local Identities*, 123 and Appendix I #15 and #16.

[312] For the legalistic aspect of curse tablets see Rodwell, *Temples, Churches, and Religion*, 87.

be the former, as *voces mysticae* have some peculiar characteristics, such as their length and repetition of syllables. There were only three examples of *charakteres*, or magical symbols, two of which come from the two golden Greek tablets, which were clearly created by someone from the Eastern Mediterranean.[313] The single remaining tablet, found at Puckeridge-Braughing, consisted only of a symbol, and the only indication that this was a curse tablet was that it had several nails driven through it.[314] This deviation from tradition may be attributed to the Britons' lack of experience with the written word. The lack of magic words and symbols may have been due to their Greco-Roman nature, as they would have had no meaning to the native Britons, therefore eschewing them in the *defixiones*. This may be another example of how native tradition trumped Roman tradition in the creation of curse tablets.

While it is clear that the curse tablets in Roman Britain were different from elsewhere in the Empire, local variation must be taken into account. It appears that the religion and culture of pre-Roman Britain may be responsible for the differences in the curse tablets. However, when other cultures were exposed to the practice of creating curse tablets, they did not result in such extreme deviation from tradition. A good comparison would be Judea, where the culture and especially the religion of the inhabitants were drastically different from that of the Romans.

Jewish and even early Christian curse tablets are common. Instead of invoking gods and sprits, they invoked God and various angels. Beyond this, however, they did not deviate much from the traditional Greco-Roman formulas. Some used Biblical imagery, such as a tablet found in Hadrumentum that entries God's intervention, writing "I invoke you, who created the heaven and the sea. I invoke you, who set aside the righteous. I invoke you, who divided the staff in the sea."[315] Despite this holy imagery, the petitioner was demanding to love of a woman, just like so many curse tablets from around the Empire.

British traditions, both religious and secular, affected not only the traditions of Romano-Britons, but Roman immigrants. The Romans taught the Britons how to construct the curse tablets, but the practice was given a distinctive British flavor. The curse tablets in Britain were almost exclusively interested in justice, possibly as a result of flaws in the judicial system. They also tended not to adhere to Mediterranean formulae, they didn't contain *voces mysticae*, and fewer tablets were folded and nailed down than elsewhere in the Empire. The native

---

[313] Appendix I #71 and #97.

[314] Appendix I #101.

[315] Gager, *Curse Tablets and Binding Spells from the Ancient World*, 113.

British population may have initiated these changes, but the Roman immigrants followed the quickly established conventions of British curse tablets. The Bath curse tablets show that a mixture of Romans and Britons created *defixiones*, yet it in most cases it is impossible to tell the tablets written by Britons and Romans apart. How the changes to the curse tablet conventions came about is unclear, but it is clear that curse tablets were not merely transported to Britain, they were transformed, and the end result was embraced by both Romans and Britons.

Chapter 5: The Physical World of the Romano-Britons

*I give to the god Maglus him who did wrong from the slave quarters. I give
him who did theft the cloak from the slave quarters, who stole the cloak of
Servandus: Silvester, Rigomandus, Senilis, Venustinus, Vorvena,
Calaminus, Felicianus, Rufaedo, Vendicina, Ingeniunus, Iuventius, Alocus,
Cennosus, Germanus, Sendo, Cunovendus, Regalis, Nigella, Senicianus. I
give that the god Maglus before the ninth day take away him who stole the
cloak of Servandus.*[316]

Servandus' curse tablet concerning the theft of his cloak is just one of the
many tablets that relate to the personal effects of the Romano-Britons. This tablet
gives not only insight into the value of clothing, but suggests the number of
inhabitants of his household and possibly the extent of literacy in Roman Britain.
While the information concerned in the curse tablets can be used to understand
the spiritual underpinnings of the Romano-Britons, it can also give us a greater
understanding into the physical world of Roman Britain, including the great
wealth attested to in some of the *defixiones*. The information in the curse tablets
can be added to the archeological data to better describe the physical changes
that Roman rule brought to Britain.

Whether it was from different needs or different beliefs, the curses in Britain
were different than those from the rest of the Empire. The absence of certain
types of curse tablets is as important as the ones that were found in Britain. By
far the most common type of *defixiones* were attempts to regain stolen
possessions and get revenge on the thief. These 'justice' tablets comprise the
entire Bath cache and the majority of the tablets outside of Bath with a stated
purpose. Most have a similar phrasing, much like this one from Bath: "I have
given to the goddess Minerva Sulis the thief who stole my hooded cloak, be he
slave or free, man or woman. Let him not redeem this gift except with his
blood."[317] Both the objects stolen and the reason for turning to magic to solve the
problem should be addressed.

There are many scenarios that could account for the high number of theft
tablets. There may have been a high crime rate, due to either a breakdown of
British society upon the conquest of the Romans and increased population and
wealth. There may have been ineptitude on the part of, or distrust of, the Roman

---

[316] Appendix I #84.

[317] Appendix I #18.

officials, which made many Romano-Britons turn to alternative sources of justice, the gods. Seven of the tablets gave the name or names of suspects, and many of the tablets that were lists of names could have been potential suspect lists, suggesting that even when a victim suspected who was responsible for the theft, they were unable to do anything about it.[318] There is so little epigraphic evidence in Roman Britain that it is impossible to say which scenario was responsible for the increased need of theft curse tablets.

These potential reasons for the high number of theft and justice curse tablets revolve around the society of Roman Britain. The native British society may have broken down and the Romano-British society that replaced it was unable to cope. The societal structure of Britain before the Roman conquest is one of the most difficult areas to ascertain. Britain before the conquest is often referred to as being Celtic, and although the language was indeed a Celtic tongue, this does not mean that there was an identical culture shared by all those who spoke Celtic, such as the Gauls.[319] There was no homogeneity even among the peoples of Britain. [320] The landscape of the island made it difficult to have large political units and similarly they did not have the same culture or societal structure amongst the many tribes of Britain. While Britain is often compared to Gaul in culture, it would perhaps be more apt to compare it to Iberia, where there was a myriad of cultures and identities.[321]

The pre-Roman British society was far more rural than it was to become under Roman rule, but the Romans had little interest in changing the society in the lands they conquered. However, the Romans very presence changed British society a great deal. The most noticeable change for the native Britons would have been the creation of towns and cities. Many Britons would still continue to live in small agricultural communities, but some would move to cities or enroll in the army and be posted in urbanized areas. The Britons may have viewed these Roman creations as proof of the power of the Empire, but it is hard to ascertain how the Britain coped with their changing landscape.[322] There was also an astonishing diversity of rural settlements in Roman Britain, including those of the native variety and Roman-style villas.[323] While many areas had an increasing

---

[318] Appendix I #84, #85, #93, #98, #105, #108, and #110.

[319] Nora K. Chadwick, *Celtic Britain* (New York: Frederick A. Praeger, 1964), 19.

[320] Haselgrove, "Society and Polity in Late Iron Age Britain," 12.

[321] Keay, "Innovation and Adaption," 292

[322] Petts, "Landscape and Cultural Identity in Roman Britain," in *Cultural Identity in the Roman Empire*, ed. Ray Laurence and Joanne Berry (London and New York: Routledge, 1998), 87-88.

[323] A. L. F. Rivet, "Summing Up: The Classification of Minor Towns and Related Settlements," in

population, some locations that had had connections to the former states dwindled. The long inhabited hill fort of Danebury appears to have been abandoned during the Roman period.[324]

Along with urbanization came the trappings of Roman urban life, and an increased crime rate. The Romans constructed roads, baths, forums, temples, and arenas. By the time of the conquest, Roman engineers could plan these structures quickly and efficiently. Some of these structures were created extremely early in the occupation, such as the forum of London, which was complete when Boudicca sacked the city in 60 C.E.[325] Just because this was the edge of the Empire did not mean that these urban structures lacked the style of buildings in Rome. Engineers and artisans took great pains to impress visitors to the public buildings. The main hall in the baths at Wroxeter was 240 feet long and 65 feet wide.[326] One notable absence in the landscape was the lack of a circus, although there is some suggestion there might have been one near the discovery of an Epona relief in Wroxeter.[327] Chariot racing was the most popular entertainment in the Roman Empire, equitable to football in Europe. To not have a single arena dedicated to it would have been highly unusual.

The increase in urban life would have helped increase crime, but dissatisfaction with and alienation from Romano-British society would have also increased crime. An ancient Briton would have identified himself or herself in a number of ways, but primarily through family bonds, not as a member of a political unit. This made the Roman idea of citizenship a difficult concept for the Britons to understand. Roman citizenship was restricted in early period to some immigrants and those who received citizenship as a part of a treaty.[328] In the original four *coloniae*, which were cities created for Roman citizens, there were a few natives alongside the hordes of Roman citizens from all the provinces. Many of the legionaries that were sent to Britain were not from Italy, and the ones which were, came from the Celtic regions in Northern Italy, so there was not much of a 'Latin' culture in these places.[329]

The 'Small Towns' of Roman Britain: Papers Presented to Conference, Oxford 1975, ed. Warwick Rodwell and Trevor Rowley (Oxford: British Archaeological Reports, 1975), 111.

[324] Barry Cunliffe, *Danebury: An Iron Age Hillfort in Hampshire*, vol. I (London: Council for British Archaeology, 1984), 12

[325] B. J. Philp, Ralph Merrifield, Geoffrey Dannell, Peter Couldrey, M. Y. Stant, and Wendy Williams, "The Forum of Roman London: Excavations of 1968-9," *Britannia* 8 (1977): 1.

[326] Philip Barker, "Excavations on the Site of the Baths Basilica at Wroxeter 1966-1974: An Interim Report," *Britannia* 6 (1975): 106.

[327] Alcock, "The People," 79.

[328] Allason-Jones, *Daily Life in Roman Britain*, 11-12.

The population of Britain grew under Roman rule, and peaked between the second and fourth centuries, depending on the area.[330] This population growth was aided by advancements in agricultural production which slowly increased the native population, but the numerous military personnel that were stationed in Britain had a much more sudden demographic impact. Estimates of Britain's population range from one to two million, of which 63,000 would have been active army personnel.[331] Except in the forts, Romans would not have made up the majority the population in any area. Even in the *coloniae* more than half of the residents would not have been Romans. They would be craftsmen, artisans, soldiers' families, and servants.[332] Urban commercial and industrial workers were predominantly British.[333] There were also many immigrants that came to the cities which added to their cosmopolitan nature. A doctor from the Greek East and a sculptor from Palmyra would have felt equally at home as the Roman veterans in the cities of Britain.[334]

The influx of new people and changes in British society may have resulted in a high crime rate and/or alienation with Roman authorities. However there is no clear proof of this, and Gaul, which had a similar shift in society with the Roman conquest did not have a disproportionate number of theft and justice tablets. Perhaps the combination of societal changes and the Briton's spiritual beliefs combined to create the unique circumstances in which these *defixiones* were viewed as a perfect solution. However, without better epigraphic evidence about crime in Britain, this must be relegated to the realm of speculation.

The reasons for the high number of theft tablets aside, the theft tablets can reveal much about the material world of the Romano-Britons. Theft was the cause for the curses in 53% of all curse tablets and 85% of tablets with a stated purpose.[335] The types of items reported stolen showed what Romano-Britons held dear. Nine household items are amongst the stolen items that their owners begged to have restored to them. Among them are items that could be made domestically or were imported. One item that would have been locally made was a rug or blanket. The Bath tablet that records its theft demands that the thief

---

[329] Birley, *The People of Roman Britain*, 116.

[330] Michael Fulford, "Economic Structures" in *A Companion to Roman Britain,* ed. Malcolm Todd (Malden, MA: Blackwell Publishing, 2004), 311-312.

[331] Alcock, "The People," 74

[332] Webster, *Celtic Religion in Roman Britain*, 80

[333] Shotter, *Roman Britain*, 75.

[334] Shotter, *Roman Britain*, 75

[335] See Appendix II, table 2.

pay for his crime in blood, so the owner was obviously quite attached to it and/or particularly vindictive.[336] The creation of rugs, blankets, and other textiles, would have taken place in the home in Roman Britain, as it would have in prehistoric Britain.

The most common items reported stolen by the curse tablets were textiles, specifically, articles of clothing. Despite the stereotype of Celts running around naked before they were conquered by Rome, textiles had long and surprisingly well documented history in Britain. The pre-Roman Britons' textiles were made mostly from domesticated sheep's wool.[337] The changes in clothing in Britain, or lack thereof, echo the larger societal changes that occurred with the Roman conquest. Before the conquest, fabric production was highly sophisticated and the clothing fit the climate. [338] The invasion did little to impact the garb worn by the average Briton, either in style or quality.[339] Latin style garments and luxurious fabrics were introduced, but were restricted to the upper classes and often only donned on special occasions. [340] Likewise, the fabric of British society remained, and while the outward appeared of Romanization could be viewed in some, native traditions remained at the core of Britain.

The most popular material for clothing remained wool, but flax, hemp, and animal hair were all used.[341] The 'Gallic coat' was the most popular garment in Roman Britain, while traditional Roman garb was only used for official occasions.[342] Another popular garment was the simple sleeved shirt, which probably originated from Celtic clothing.[343] Women's clothing was conservative and echoed the clothes worn by their ancestors before the conquest.[344] Only later did the Britain start to have a "greater awareness of how the rest of the Empire dressed."[345] The Romano-British method of spinning and weaving clothing was also more attuned to the Celtic tradition than the Roman tradition. British

---

[336] Appendix I #26.

[337] Coles and Harding, *The Bronze Age in Europe*, 477.

[338] John Peter Wild, "Textiles and Dress," in *A Companion to Roman Britain*, ed. Malcolm Todd (Malden, MA: Blackwell Publishing, 2004), 299.

[339] John Peter Wild, *Textile Manufacture in the Northern Roman Provinces* (Cambridge: Cambridge University Press, 1970), 1.

[340] Wild, "Textiles and Dress," 303.

[341] Wild, "Textiles and Dress," 299.

[342] Wild, "Textiles and Dress," 302.

[343] Wild, "Textiles and Dress," 302.

[344] Wild, "Textiles and Dress," 305.

[345] Wild, "Textiles and Dress," 306.

spinners favored right-spinning, as did those in Gaul.[346] In both fabric boarders and selvedge, British weaving techniques were different from those in the Mediterranean basin.[347] However, the technology employed by the Romano-British was similar in most respects to their Continental Roman counterparts. Archeological finds pertaining to weaving and clothes making were similar in Britain and continental provinces.[348] It appears that the Romano-British started to breed sheep for their wool while their popularity as a food source decreased.[349]

Fourteen *defixiones* mention stolen clothing, making up 21% of all theft tablets. By far the most commonly stolen item was a cloak, with eight reported stolen.[350] These were probably the Gallic coats noted above, which were essential daily wear. Due to the expense and necessity of these garments, owners were eager to get them back. All segments of the population appeared to have worn these, including a Bath patron who wrote: "Docilianus son of Brucerus to the most holy goddess Sulis. I curse him who has stolen my hooded cloak, whether man or woman, slave or free, that . . . the goddess Sulis inflicts death upon . . ."[351] Another item stolen was gloves, with three reports of their theft.[352] Two tunics were reported stolen, one of them a bathing tunic.[353] Lastly, there were one report each of a stolen cap and a pair of gaiters.[354] With the exception of the tunics and gaiters, all of these were cold weather clothing, understandable in such a climate, and necessities for surviving a winter in good health.

There were several agricultural items that were listed as stolen. The owners' desire to retrieve these items is not surprising, since the backbone of the British economy was agriculture, both before and after the Roman conquest. For much of Britain's prehistory, agriculture was at subsistence levels.[355] Iron Age fields were generally square and small, about a fifth of a hectare, which was what a man could plow in a day.[356] Despite Strabo's claim that there was neither horticulture nor animal husbandry, most ancient Britons appeared to have had

---

[346] Wild, *Textile Manufacture*, 44.

[347] Wild, "The Textile Industries of Roman Britain," 15-18.

[348] Wild, *Textile Manufacture*, 123-142.

[349] Wild, "The Textile Industries of Roman Britain," 2-4.

[350] Appendix I #7, #18, #38, #47, #58, #75, #84, and #115.

[351] Appendix I #7.

[352] Appendix I #23, #104, and #119.

[353] Appendix I #38 and #57.

[354] Appendix I #75 and #104.

[355] Wacher, *Roman Britain*, 106.

[356] John Wacher, *A Portrait of Roman Britain* (London: Routledge, 2000), 45.

both.[357]   Domesticated sheep and cattle were raised along with domesticated staple crops, and wild animals, such as deer helped round out the ancient British diet.[358] The shift from substance to commercial agriculture occurred once there was a market for the excess grain. Caesar's requisition of corn during his Gallic campaign likely laid foundation for agricultural trade.[359]

Agriculture still dominated the economic landscape in Roman Britain. While there had been a trade in grain during the pre-Roman period, the agricultural output could not sustain a large, non-producing population. Therefore, food supplies were not sufficient to feed the army during the conquest, and were imported from the Continent.[360] Agricultural methods improved over time as the Romans introduced higher-quality ploughs, spades, and scythes.[361] Few crops were introduced to Britain at the time, however more spelt and root vegetables were grown in the Roman period.[362]   The Roman villa, the embodiment of Roman agriculture, found a place in the British countryside. There were around 1000 villas in Roman Britain, although the presence of villas did not mean that all Romano-British agricultural workers abandoned the simple farms of their ancestors. [363] Small Iron Age farmsteads still existed, sometimes within sight of grand Roman villas.[364]

Several theft tablets related to the importance of agriculture, and they demanded harsh penalties against the thieves of agricultural tools that were invaluable and expensive to farmers. Tools that the Romans introduced into Britain were highly prized, and when a farmer had his ploughshare stolen he demanded, "if anyone has stolen Civilis' ploughshare I ask that he lay down his life in the temple."[365] A tablet from Uley asks for the return of a much needed draught animal, "he begs the god Mercury that they may neither have health . . . unless they repay me promptly for the animal they have stolen."[366] Other stolen

---

[357] Strabo, *The Geography of Strabo.* vol. 1, trans. H. C. Hamilton (London: G. Bell and Sons, 1912), V.2.

[358] J. M. Coles and A. F. Harding, *The Bronze Age in Europe* (London: Methuen & Co., 1979), 477.

[359] Wacher, *Roman Britain*, 106.

[360] Fulford, "Economic Structures," 314.

[361] Wacher, *Roman Britain*, 107.

[362] Wacher, *A Portrait of Roman Britain*, 47.

[363] Wacher, *A Portrait of Roman Britain*, 49.

[364] Shotter, *Roman Britain*, 77.

[365] Appendix I #37. Original Latin: "*si [qui]s vome/rem Civilis / involavit / ut an[imam] / suua[m] in tem/plo deponat / [si n]o[n] vom/[erem] . . .ub/ . . .[si se]rvus / si liber si li/bertinus . . / unan . . o / finem faci/[a]m.*"

items include and axe, a bridle, a mule or millstone, and a horse blanket.[367] The implements and animals reported stolen in the curse tablets show that agriculture occurred on a great scale in Roman Britain and the tools and animals involved in agriculture were precious to farmers.

Table 5: In Curse Tablets Related to Theft, Which Items Were Stolen

	From Bath	From Outside of Bath	Total
Money	3 3%	5 16%	8 12%
Clothing	9 25%	5 16%	14 21%
Jewelry	2 6%	3 10%	5 7%
Household Items	4 10%	5 16%	9 14%
Other	3 8%	7 23%	9 14%
Unknown	15 42%	6 20%	21 32%

Household items accounted for 14% of stated thefts, and most of these items were metal. This could indicate that the Britons skilled metalworking was still prized by the Romano-Britons. Pre-Roman Britons were experts in metalworkers, and most of their art was crafted in metal.[368] Much of this metalwork was practical as well as beautiful. Items such as swords, shields bosses, mirrors, and brooches were often ornately decorated. Gold was the favored medium in Celtic jewelry and indicated wealth, but British art has been found in a variety of metals. The technique used by Celtic metalworkers was called *repoussé*, which consisted of casting and engraving on metal.[369] This work was extremely detailed, and Celtic metalworkers were well known for their

---

[366] Appendix I #108. Original Latin: "*Deo Mercurio / Cenacus queritur / de Vitalino et Nat/lino filio ipsius d[e] / iumento quod erap/tum est. Erogat / deum Mercurium / ut nec ante sa/nitatem.*" Reverese: "*habeant nisi / nisi repraese[n]/taverint mihi iu/mentum quod r[a]/puerunt et deo devotionem qua[m] / ipse ab his ex/postulaverit.*"

[367] Appendix I #125, #111, #103, and #51.

[368] Henig, *The Art of Roman Britain*, 14.

[369] Henig, *The Art of Roman Britain*, 21.

talents in the ancient world. However, they either did not know how to create or did not choose to use fine wire, which was used by the Romans and utilized in Roman Britain.[370]

Some of the metal house-wares were purely utilitarian, such as the pans reported missing by three separate curse tablets.[371] Another practical item was reported stolen in Ratcliffe-on-Soar, a simple knife.[372] However, there are several examples where the stolen items were of the highly decorative, luxury nature. One example from Bath relates to a bronze vessel, which was certainly a luxury item.[373] Another tablet mentions a mirror and ten pewter vessels.[374] A silver plate reported stolen from Uley was an extraordinary luxury.[375] The combination of utilitarian and luxury items that are mentioned in the *defixiones* shows that there were are range of socio-economic groups that were using the curse tablets. It also shows that there was a certain amount of wealth in this lonely province.

The most basic housewares were not noted in the curse tablets. Neither pottery nor furniture was mentioned, but there is plenty of evidence of both of these. The pottery and furniture of Roman Britain appeared to be rooted in the Roman tradition, yet still had a British flavor. While little furniture survived from Roman Britain, the pieces that survived and the depictions on tombstones depict Roman forms, however their craftsmanship and the materials used are quintessentially British.[376] While pottery had been in use in Britain long before the appearance of the Romans, highly decorated pottery was relatively rare. Samian ware, the Classical ornamental pottery, was both imported to and made in Britain. While the Samian ware dominated the ornamental pottery trade, there were also some more Celtic styled pieces that have been unearthed.

There were five tablets where jewelry is reported stolen. Both British and Roman culture held jewelry in high regard, and the Britons, expert metalworkers that they were, had an especially rich history of jewelry-making. Jewelry was the most common application of the British metalworker's skills. As was true for the Classical world, fibula and brooches were needed to pin together clothing. They

---

[370] Catherine Johns, *The Jewellery of Roman Britain: Celtic and Classical Traditions* (Ann Arbor: University of Michigan Press, 1996), 30.

[371] Appendix I #56, 59, 73.

[372] Appendix I #104.

[373] Appendix I #19.

[374] Appendix I #75.

[375] Appendix I #120.

[376] Joan Liversidge, *Furniture in Roman Britain* (London: Alec Tiranti Ltd. 1955), 66.

ranged from the simple to incredibly complex. Along with fibula, bracelets were made in the Iron Age of Briton. Both of these works of jewelry continued to develop under Roman rule, yet they often kept their Celtic aesthetic.[377] Both glass and beaded bracelets appeared in Roman Britain, and were most likely a Roman import.[378] Bracelets were reported stolen in both Bath and Castor St. Edmund, but it is unclear if they were of native design or imported beaded design.[379] Both women's rings and earrings were Roman imports.[380] Few British women appeared to have started wearing earrings, but finger rings did gain popularity. In fact many examples of fingered rings, made of various metals and in various styles, have been found in Roman Britain.[381] In Bath, a woman named Basilia reports that her silver ring was stolen.[382] Three other curse tablets report stolen rings.[383]

Notably absent from the reports of stolen jewelry are forms that are characteristically British. This could partially be due to the decline in traditional British jewelry during the Roman period. Torcs have been viewed as a quintessentially Celtic form of ornamentation. These often massive pieces of gold neckwear were symbols of power in the Celtic world. However, by the first century B.C.E. they were no longer worn by the Celts on the Continent.[384] They did not survive much longer in Britain, and their appearance died out not long after Roman rule began, possibly because they were royal wear and the conquest negated those societal positions.[385] While it was unintentional, the Romans managed to eradicate the torc from Britain.

While the torcs all but disappeared from Roman Britain, other indigenous forms of jewelry did not. Brooches made of metal were the most popular enameled objects.[386] Unlike other jewelry, these brooches did not seem to change

---

[377] Johns, *The Jewellery of Roman Britain*, 30.

[378] Alexandra Croom, "Personal Ornament," in *A Companion to Roman Britain*, ed. Malcolm Todd (Malden, MA: Blackwell Publishing, 2004), 288 and 290.

[379] Appendix I #12 and #75.

[380] Johns, *The Jewellery of Roman Britain*, 30-31.

[381] Croom, "Personal Ornament," 295.

[382] Appendix I #14.

[383] Appendix I #93, #133, and #120.

[384] Johns, *The Jewellery of Roman Britain*, 28.

[385] Johns, *The Jewellery of Roman Britain*, 29.

[386] Henig, *The Art of Roman Britain*, 21. Celtic style brooches were also imported into Britain from other Celtic areas, see Patrick Galliou, "Three East Gaulish Brooches Found in Britain," *Britannia* 12 (1981):288-289.

with the Roman occupation. Brooches in Roman Britain, which span the period of Roman control, had designs that were either Celtic or simplistic in nature.[387] The equestrian plate brooches remained completely pre-Roman in nature, forgoing anatomical accuracy, they were extremely abstract.[388] The Britons continued to create enamels through at least the third century, until there was a general economic slow down and luxury good greatly decreased.[389] The enameled brooches, along with other enameled objects, resurged after the province was abandoned by Rome.[390] At a time when little else was created, Celtic enameled goods were still being produced as if the four century Roman occupation had never occurred. One explanation was that enameled brooches were one of the simplest and most affordable pieces of artwork a Briton could own, making them accessible to the rural population that was relatively untouched by Romanization. These un-Romanized pieces of jewelry were not mentioned in the curse tablets, perhaps because they were still being created by those who were thoroughly un-Romanized themselves.

The theft of money was often the root cause of many curse tablets. Eight tablets, 12% of theft tablets, report money stolen.[391] The amounts stolen range from 5, to an astonishing 4000, *denarii*.[392] Smaller amounts can be accounted for as pocket money or the money in one's home, but other amounts are bafflingly high. The large sums, including not only the 4000 *denarii* case, but 3000 *denarii* and others, suggest that even the elites of Romano-British society may have had difficulty in receiving justice from the authorities.[393] The large sums could be evidence of large scale trade, as these large sums would not be useful for anything else.

Trade certainly flourished in Britain with the conquest by the Romans, but there was long-distance trade even before the invasion. Most trade in prehistoric Britain took place within the Isles, but long-distance trade increased in the centuries leading up to the conquest. Pre-Roman trade routes are mostly evident due to the trade in metalwork. Areas without mineral deposits, like Kent, traded

---

[387] Sarnia A Butcher, "Enamels from Roman Britain," in *Ancient Monument and Their Interpretation: Essays Presented to A. J. Taylor,* ed. M. R. Apted, R. Gilyard-Beer, and A. D. Saunders (London: Phillimore & Co., 1977), 51-64.

[388] Butcher, "Enamels from Roman Britain," 54-56.

[389] Butcher, "Enamels from Roman Britain," 43.

[390] Henig, *The Art of Roman Britain*, 105.

[391] Appendix I #4, #5, #13, #75, #80, #81, #85, and #98.

[392] Appendix I #13 and #80.

[393] The 3000 *denarii* case refers to Appendix I #98.

with areas such as Dover and Essex to gain these valuable resources.[394] In return, stone from Kent was traded to Essex.[395] Metalwork from South-eastern Britain was exported to the Continent. British metalwork has mostly been found in Gaul, but also Spain and the Mediterranean.[396] The port at Hengistbury in Wessex was one of the main trading ports, and shows evidence of a trade in iron, copper, gold, silver, shale, and grain.[397] Strabo claimed that one of the exports of Britain was slaves.[398] Archeological evidence of collars and chains confirms that there was a slave trade in prehistoric Britain.[399] In exchange for all these goods, Britain gained access to items such as wine, olive oil, fish sauce, and grain.[400]

By the first century C.E., the British economy had ceased to rely upon bartering, and was quickly becoming involved in long-distance trade. The Roman conquest accelerated the shift from subsistence agriculture to a commercial economy, but the goods created in Britain were the same as before. While a pre-conquest Briton may have created pottery in addition to farming his land, a Roman Briton would have worked almost exclusively as a farmer or a potter. The radical shift in the political system, from tribal affiliation to living in the Roman Empire, was not felt too harshly by the average Briton, whose day-to-day work activities did not change much beyond specialization. True, now the Emperor was the biggest landowner in Britain, but how much this affected the common laborer is hard to say.[401] The same is true for the "heavy burdens" of taxation, which by some estimates was 10%.[402] Without knowing what taxes were like before Rome, it is impossible to compare the two.

One of the traded commodities in Roman Britain was lead, the traditional material for the creation of curse tablets. While many of the tablets from outside of Bath were lead, few from Bath were. While some religious reasons for this were suggested in the last chapter, there may be more practical reasons that relate to the production of lead in Britain. Along with basic agriculture, mining was one of the staples in the prehistoric British economy. Britain was blessed with mineral wealth, and the native Britons became great metalworkers centuries

---

[394] Champion, "Prehistoric Kent," 114.

[395] Champion, "Prehistoric Kent," 115.

[396] Coles and Harding, *The Bronze Age in Europe*, 482 and Fulford, "Economic Structures," 313.

[397] Cunliffe, *Wessex to 1000 AD*, 202.

[398] Strabo, *The Geography of Strabo*, vol. 2.

[399] Champion, "Prehistoric Kent," 130

[400] Fulford, "Economic Structures," 313.

[401] Faulkner, *The Decline and Fall of Roman Britain*, 74.

[402] Faulkner, *The Decline and Fall of Roman Britain*, 81.

before the conquest. One of the most important deposits was tin. In Cornwall, or *Belerium* as Diodorus called it, there were large deposits of tin which they mined and refined for export out of the area.[403] Western Britain had copper deposits, which were exported throughout the Isles.[404] Tin and copper, being the two main ingredients in bronze, were highly sought after, and were probably the main reason for traders to visit the island before the conquest. Tacitus reports that there were deposits of gold and silver, although only the latter has been shown to be found in abundance.[405] Strabo also stated that gold and silver were produced in Britain, along with iron.[406]

While the native Britons mined on a small scale, the Romans instituted a formal mining industry. Britain's mineral wealth was well known to the Romans, and they did what they could to tap these resources.[407] Lead was the most prolific mineral to come out of Romano-British mines. Lead was used for lining baths, cisterns, making water pipes and coffins.[408] Coffins with lead in them would often be made primarily of stone.[409] Coffins lined with lead were indicators of wealth and have been found in Wiveliscombe, Chillington, Bearley Farm, Ilchester Med, Ilchester, Charlton Ilchester, and Prestleigh.[410] The lead mined in Britain stayed mostly with the province, although silver, which can be extracted from lead ore, was distributed more widely.[411] The Romans encouraged the mining of both gold and lead during first century C.E.[412] It appears that the earliest site of Roman lead mining was at Charterhouse.[413] The lead mine at Lutudarum, near Matlock Bath, exported metal to the Continent.[414]

---

[403] Diodorus, *The Library of History*, vol. 3, trans. C. H. Oldfather (Cambridge, MA: Harvard University Press, 1939), v.22.1-2.

[404] Champion, "Prehistoric Kent," 115.

[405] Tacitus, *Agricola*, 12. "*Fert Britannia aurum et argentums et alia metalla, pretium victoriae.*"

[406] Strabo, *The Geography of Strabo*, vol. 2.

[407] Jean David C Boulakia, "Lead in the Roman World," *American Journal of Archaeology* 76, no. 2 (1972): 140 and Caius Julius Solinus, *Collectanea Rerum Memorabilium*, XXXIV.30ff and Pliny the Elder, *Natural History*, vol. 4, ed. H. Rackham (London: William Heinmann Ltd., 1968), 34.49.

[408] F. R. Pearson, *Roman Yorkshire* (East Ardsley, UK: EP Publishing, 1973), 162.

[409] F. R. Pearson, *Roman Yorkshire*, 153.

[410] Warwick Rodwell, ed. *Temples, Churches and Religion: Recent Research in Roman Britain with a Gazetteer of Romano-Celtic Temples in Continental Europe* (Oxford: BAR British Series 775, 1980), 341.

[411] Fulford, "Economic Structures," 317-318.

[412] Fulford, "Economic Structures," 317.

[413] James Dyer, *Southern England: An Archeological Guide, the Prehistoric and Roman Remains* (Park Ridge, N.J.: Noyes Press, 1973), 243.

The lead industry declined in the early third century, by which time the iron industry took on added importance.[415]

It is clear that Britain did not lack access to lead, so the question of its use in the Bath tablets is not explained that easily. While many of the tablets found in Britain outside of Bath are lead, very few – seven to be exact – of the Bath tablets are lead.[416] Most of the Bath tablets are alloys that include lead, such as the pewter dish found in the springs at Bath.[417] The pewter and other tin alloys had similar physical qualities as lead, so it is understandable if individuals found them an acceptable substitute to lead sheeting if it was not immediately available. These were probably cheaper than pure lead sheeting, but it does not explain the extreme deviation from tradition. Pure tin and bronze tablets have also been discovered at Bath.[418]

Both lead and tin were found in the areas not far from Bath, so the choice to use tin alloy was unlikely to have been because of the availability of tin and lead. There may have been other economic factors at work. The tin/lead alloyed sheets may have been sold by temple officials or other local merchants for use as curse tablets. The number of *defixiones* found in the spring was such that money could be made on the sale of curse tablet materials. Since anyone depositing a curse tablet into the spring had to go through the temple, priests may have found that selling cheap scraps of tin alloy was an easy way to make money.

Bath aside, lead was used in most of the *defixiones* from around Britain. 93% of curse tablets outside of Bath were written on lead. Not only was this the traditional material for curse tablet and easy to find, it was already an established material to write upon. Lead was the most common material for labels and seals.[419] Lead was easy to attain, either legally or illegally. Sheets of lead could be stolen from several locations. Coffins were often lined in thin sheets of lead.[420] Within a stone coffin found in Winterton there was a lead sheet lining the coffin that was 1/8-3/16 of an inch thick.[421] Such thin sheets would be perfect for inscribing. Collingwood has suggested that lead sheeting from

---

[414] F. R. Pearson, *Roman Yorkshire*, 72.

[415] Fulford, "Economic Structures," 317-318 and F. R. Pearson, *Roman Yorkshire*, 165.

[416] See Appendix II, table 4 for more information.

[417] Appendix I #3.

[418] Tomlin, "The Curse Tablets," 133.

[419] Collingwood, *Roman Inscriptions of Britain* I #2410.1-2411.311.

[420] McWhirr, *Romano-British Cemeteries at Circencester*, microfiche 2-e03.

[421] Ian M. Stead, *Excavations at Winterton Roman Villa and other Roman Sites in North Lincolnshire* (London: Her Majesty's Stationary Office, 1976), 289.

houses was also used.[422]

While the material upon which the curse was written was important, the actual words written are far more significant. The curse tablets can enlighten us about literacy in Roman Britain in a way few other sources can. Latin was known amongst the traders of the southern coast of England centuries before the conquest, but in 43 C.E. it became the official language of the land. When Agricola was governor of the province, he created schools for the sons of chieftains, which taught the reading, writing, and speaking of Latin.[423] Latin was used by upper classes, who were mainly Roman, and urbanities, who needed to interact with Romans. However Celtic survived for centuries in more rural areas.[424] Without knowledge of basic Latin, a Briton could not join the army, become a merchant or an artisan, or live in an urban area. [425] Therefore, over the centuries Latin became more common in the communications between native Britons.[426] While there were immigrants and soldiers from the Greek East, their populations were small and it is safe to say most native Greek speakers in Britain were also fluent in Latin.

The evidence suggests that Latin was spoken slightly differently in Britain than it would have been in Rome or any other province. These differences mainly pertain to vowel sounds, and although they made British Latin different, it was still comprehendible to other Latin speakers.[427] Some of these spoken differences may be responsible for the spelling discrepancies on the curse tablets. Although linguistics may have been different in Britain, Britain was not a backwater. The Vindolanda tablets contained several rarely used Latin words, indicating that the Romano-British had an extensive and sophisticated vocabulary.[428]

The ancient Britons did not have a written language, at least not one which has ever been discovered.[429] The transition from an oral tradition to a literate culture proved difficult, and it initially appeared that literacy was never very high in Britain.[430] One way of establishing this is by looking at the inscriptions

---

[422] Collingwood, *Roman Inscriptions of Britain* I #7.

[423] Tacitus, *Agricola* 21.

[424] Harris, *Ancient Literacy*, 183 and 268.

[425] Allason-Jones, *Daily Life in Roman Britain*, 20.

[426] F. R. Pearson, *Roman Yorkshire*, 149.

[427] Eric P. Hamp, "Social Gradience in British Spoken Latin," *Britannia* 6 (1975): 151-152.

[428] J. N. Adams, "The New Vindolanda Writing-Tablets," *The Classical Quarterly*, New Series 53, no. 2 (2003): 530ff.

[429] Harris, *Ancient Literacy*, 183.

found in Britain. Monumental inscriptions occurred at a much lower rate in Britannia than almost any other province. There were only 5.7 inscriptions per 1000 square kilometers. The lowest was Mauretania Tingitana with 3.3 and the highest was Africa Proconsularis with 127.3.[431] The inscriptions show great range in lettering styles, suggesting that epigraphers were drafted from around the Empire.[432]

Although there are few monuments in Britain, evidence from Vindolanda and Carlisle suggest that there was high literacy, at least in the military.[433] There were clerks who were attached to the army whose duty was to keep records of all the soldiers.[434] But beyond the clerks, many other soldiers were literate. Literacy was necessary to get off the bottom rung of the military ladder, so many soldiers, including auxiliaries who hoped to command, were literate.[435]

The wooden writing tablets found in Vindolanda and Carlisle were primarily written in Latin cursive. This cursive was the same as was found in other areas of the Empire in the same period.[436] While the cursive was the same, the linguistics was not. They showed that the writers came from diverse backgrounds and social strata.[437] The small changes that occurred to Latin in Britain found their way into some of these writing tablets, and occasionally they occurred in monuments.[438] Writing did not appear to be a rare occurrence, reserved for official epistles or poetic works. The Vindolanda tablets show that even trivial matters, such as spindles and corn, were the cause for correspondence.[439]

The curse tablets follow much in the same vein as the Vindolanda tablets. All

---

[430] Harris, *Ancient Literacy*, 270.

[431] Harris, *Ancient Literacy*, 268.

[432] John Horsley, *Britannia Romana or the Roman Antiquities of Britain* Newcastle-upon-Tyne: Frank Graham, 1974), 189.

[433] Personal letters have also been found in London, see J. W. Brailsford, "Roman Writing-Tablets from London," *The British Museum Quarterly* 12, no. 2 (1954):40 & Eric G. Turner and Otto Skutsch, "A Roman Writing-Tablet from London," *The Journal of Roman Studies* 50 (1960):110.

[434] David J. Breeze, *Roman Frontiers in Britain* (London: Bristol Classical Press, 2007), 78.

[435] Allason-Jones, *Daily Life in Roman Britain*, 20.

[436] R. S. O. Tomlin, "Roman Manuscripts from Carlisle: The Ink-Written Tablets" *Britannia* 29 (1998): 34 and Bowman, *The Roman Writing Tablets from Vindolanda*, 25.

[437] Alan K. Bowman and J. David Thomas, *Vindolanda: The Latin Writing Tablets* (Gloucester, UK: Alan Sutton Publishing, 1983), 72.

[438] J. C. Mann, "Spoken Latin in Britain as Evidenced in the Inscriptions" *Britannia* 2 (1971): 218ff.

[439] Alan K. Bowman and J. David Thomas, "New Writing-Tablets from Vindolanda" *Britannia* 27 (1996): 326-327.

segments of the population appear to be addressed. From Leicester there is a slave demanding the return of his cloak.[440] Meanwhile, in Farely Heath, there is a wealthy man asking for his 4000 *denarii* back.[441] Out of the 1600 curse tablet in existence, over 10% were found in the tiny province of Britannia, which suggests not only that curse tablets were popular in Britain, but that a sizable proportion of Romano-Britons were on some level literate. Since there is no evidence of professional magicians in Britain, along with the personal nature of some of these tablets, especially the vicious ones, many of the tablets were probably written with little or no help. The two Celtic tablets would not have been written in Celtic if a Latin speaker had been there to write it for them.[442] The lack of monumental inscriptions is deceiving. While the Roman administration did not have a vested interest in promoting the literacy of the Romano-Britons, the residents of Britain appeared to have the desire and ability to learn to read and write.

Several of the tablets contain poor spelling which make it unclear as to what is trying to be said. Some of the Romano-British *defixiones* were simply illegible scribbles on lead. The writers of these tablets were probably not literate, but understood the importance of scribbling something down for the gods to act upon. For other tablets, there are clear marks, but they were not the work of a practiced hand. There is disagreement between Adams and Tomlin about the reading of several of these tablets.[443] Poor grammar, poor handwriting, and misspellings do not necessarily mean that the authors of the tablets were of the under classes or not native speakers. [444] However, this does indicate that individuals from wide range of socio-economic backgrounds visited the temple of Bath and created curse tablets.

While names were an essential part of any curse, the hundreds of names given in the British tablets can only reveal so much. About half of curse tablet names derive from Celtic and the other half are Roman, both in and outside of Bath.[445] This surprisingly high number of Celtic names suggests that areas with many curse tablets, such as Bath and Uley, were a mix of Romans and native Britons who freely associated. Given that some of the Celtic names were the names of the curse tablet creators, this suggests that the creation of curse tablets

---

[440] Appendix I #84.

[441] Appendix I #80.

[442] Appendix I #31 and #33.

[443] Adams, "British Latin," 24.

[444] Adams, "British Latin," 24.

[445] Tomlin, "The Curse Tablets," 98-97.

was quickly embraced by the native population. The most significant tablet that proves this is the Bath tablet that not only contained Celtic names but was written in Celtic.[446]

Names can shed light on the changing identity of the Britons. The Celtic Britons had only one name, their personal name.[447] In the Roman tradition the *nomen*, or family name, was most likely to reveal a family's origin, but British citizen often took the name of the Emperor who gave them citizenship.[448] Therefore their family name was not as meaningful to Britons as it was to other Romans. The curse tablets and other epigraphic evidence shows little use of mixed Celtic/Latin names, although in areas such as Gaul they were far more common.[449] The number of Celtic and Latin names in the Bath tablets is a matter of dispute, since many of the names were abbreviated or cut short by decay. Mullen counted 77 Celtic names and 70 Latin names.[450] Celtic personal names decreased over time, but prominent Celtic names remained in Britain through the sixth century.[451] Apparently a Celtic name did not hold any stigma in Roman society, as the first bishop of Rouen in the third century was from Britain and had the Celtic derived name Mellonus.[452]

The names listed on the curse tablets do not establish the ethnicity or origin of the persons involved with the *defixiones*. Celtic and Latin names were often combined in the tablets, but this occurred throughout the Roman British era. The tablets prove hard to date, only by analyzing the various styles of script is it possible to give a date to the tablets, and it appears that most of the Bath tablets were written between 175 C.E. and 400 C.E.[453] Therefore, most of the tablets were written after the time in which all Britons became Roman citizens, at which time they adopted Latin names. Separating those from the province who had adopted a new name and those from outside the province is almost impossible. Furthering the confusion, Celtic names do not necessarily indicate a native

---

[446] Appendix I #31.

[447] Allason-Jones, *Daily Life in Roman Britain*, 19 and Alex Mullen, "Linguistic Evidence for 'Romanization': Continuity and Change in Romano-British Onomastics; A Study of the Epigraphic Record with Particular Reference to Bath," *Britannia* 38 (2007): 40.

[448] Allason-Jones, *Daily Life in Roman Britain*, 18-19.

[449] Mullen, "Linguistic Evidence for 'Romanization'," 42.

[450] Mullen, "Linguistic Evidence for 'Romanization'," 51-52.

[451] Martin Henig, *The Heirs of King Verica: Culture and Politics in Roman Britain* (Stroud, UK: Tempus Publishing, 2002), 128.

[452] Birely, *The People of Roman Britain*, 153.

[453] Burgess, "Formulaic Construction in Curse Tablets from Roman Britain," 4-5.

Briton. They could refer to people who immigrated from the Celtic areas of the Continent or the non-Roman areas of Briton such as Ireland. While the linguistic roots of the names found in the curse tablets can be deceiving, it is clear that interaction between Britons and Romans was common in the urban areas where these tablets were primarily found. It is also clear from the names and other information contained within the *defixiones* that curse tablets were deemed useful by the Britons.

Many Romano-British curse tablets consisted only of names, which is peculiar. While curse tablets were originally short, giving only the names of the person(s) cursed, by the first century, most had evolved into much longer curses. In the second and third centuries C.E., many curses were quite extensive, such as the eighteen line diatribe found in the well of the Athenian agora.[454] It is difficult to ascertain the length of most of the British curse tablets because they are rarely preserved intact. The fragmentary tablets suggest that the average Romano-British curse tablet was relatively brief, but not remarkably so. The brevity of the British tablets is probably related to the lack of long magical formulae being used, not due to the inability of the Romano-Britons to write long tablets.

Most written sources from Roman Britain, including the curse tablets, were in Latin. This is not surprising considering that Britannia, was in the Latin West and was inhabited by legionaries that were primarily from Latin speaking areas.[455] There are three tablets that are not in Latin. Two can barely be called curse tablets since they are of the protective nature and are in Greek.[456] But the most fascinating by far is a tablet found in Bath that was in Celtic.[457] This tablet is fragmentary, but several Celtic words can be discerned from it: ". . . storehouse . . . / . . . stole from me, a son of the fosterage of Cimluci. . . / . . . You make claim upon . . ."[458] It is clearly a theft tablet, just like all the other Bath tablets, and other than the language used, it does not deviate from the other Bath tablets. The occurrence of the Celtic tablet proves that even native Britons who were not fully Romanized became literate and embraced ideas such as curse tablets. Bilingual tablets in Greek and Latin have been found in places such as Cuenca, but none have been discovered in Britain.[459] Similarly, a bilingual charm has been found

---

[454] David Jordon, "A Curse Tablet from a Well in the Athenian Agora," *Zeitschrift für Papyrologie und Epigraphick* 19 (1975): 245-246.

[455] Birley, *The People of Roman Britain*, 116.

[456] Appendix I #71 and #97.

[457] Appendix I #31.

[458] Tanslation by Mark Bradley.

[459] Jamie B. Cubera, Marta Sierra Delage, and Isabel Velázquez, "A Bilingual Curse Tablet from

in Norfolk, but it appears that the magical uses of Greek in Britain did not include curse tablets.[460]

In addition to adding to our understanding of the spiritual and religious world of the Romano-Britons, the curse tablets can give greater insight into the day to day world of Roman Britons. It is clear theft was a problem that the Romano-British believed could be solved in part by the use of curse tablets. Roman Britons depended on, and treasured, items that originated both in the Roman and Celtic areas. The people who made the *defixiones* in Roman Britain were similarly diverse. Literacy was more widespread than some historians initially thought, and even Celts wrote down their language in curse tablet form.

Barchín del Hoyo (Cuenca, Spain)," *Zeitschrift für Papyrologie und Empigraphik* 125 (1999): 280.
[460] Tomlin, "A Bilingual Roman Charm for Health and Victory," 259.

Conclusions: Britons in the Roman Empire

Rome took Britain from prehistory into history. The first named inhabitants of this island emerge in the pages of Julius Caesar. . . . Soon most of the Britons were to acquiesce in Roman domination.[461]

"Curse tablet" is somewhat of a misnomer for the British *defixiones*. A curse, by modern linguistic standards, insinuates a negative outcome for the cursed individual or community.[462] The best known curses are Biblical, and include curses intended to provoke divine intercession or revenge.[463] Classical curse tablets include some very vindictive prayers, but also pleas for love and justice. In the majority of the British curse tablets, the theft of a treasured item resulted in the creation of curse tablets by the victim of the theft, in an attempt to get their property back and punish the criminal.

The Roman Britons, especially those in Bath, created curse tablets differently than the rest of the Empire. Unlike the curse tablets of democratic Athens, that concerned legal and political proceedings which reflected only a privileged few, the curse tablets in Britain reflected society as a whole. In this way they are like the North African *defixiones*, where the beloved sport of chariot racing spawned a slew of chariot race related curses.[464] The British tablets were almost exclusively concerned with theft, mostly of items, but sometimes the theft was indeterminate. Theft occurs in all social groups, which was shown in the *defixiones*.

The tablets paint a portrait of Britons Romanizing on their own terms, adapting practices that they approved of and understood, while eschewing others. It is clear that Britons who lived in the cities were exposed to far more Roman religious practices than their rural cousins. While some native deities and rituals were influenced by cults from around the Empire, other practices and gods remained untouched. Traditions relating to the curse tablets such as piercing the lead tablet and burying it with the dead were mostly ignored in

---

[461] Birley, *The People of Roman Britain*, 11.

[462] Herbert Chanan Brichto, *The Problem of 'Curse' in the Hebrew Bible* (Philadelphia: Society of Biblical Literature, 1963), 1.

[463] Brichto, *The Problem of 'Curse' in the Hebrew Bible*, 7. i.e. Exodus 22:27

[464] M. W. C. Hassall, "Altars, Curses and Other Epigraphic Evidence," in *Temples, Churches and Religion: Recent Research in Roman Britain, ed.* Warwick Rodwell (Oxford: British Archeological Reports, 1980), 86.

Briton, not only by the native Britons but by the Romans. Other concepts, such as appealing to the god for justice became incredibly popular and surpassed the rest of the Empire in abundance.

The high number theft tablets suggests that there may have been some problems in receiving justice from the Roman authorities. While there was little conflict within society after the initial conquest, traditional authority figures disappeared, along with social order. The theft tablets indicate that either there was an increase of crime or that the officials in charge of law enforcement were not trusted. Either way, it was a problem that threatened the stability of the native society. Although the Britons acclimated their religion to Rome, their society was irrevocably altered, and it could not withstand the departure of Rome.[465] The rapid destruction of Roman Britain upon the official abandonment of the province is shocking and would not have occurred if the local British society had been strong.

When the Romans abandoned Britain, the use of curse tablets stopped, but some of the fundamentals of the *defixiones* remained. The use of curse tablets subsided in the fifth century C.E. throughout the Empire, yet the language of the curse tablets survived into the medieval period. The similarity of medieval curses and those found on curse tablets suggests that the ancient curses did not disappear with the appearance of Christianity; they just took on a verbal form.[466] At the very least, the centuries of using curse tablets enabled made cursing a part of the cultural lexicon of Britain.[467] In 665 the Welsh Bishop Euddogwy cursed the king, with the words quite similar to those found in the *defixiones*, "May his days be few and may his sons be orphans and his wife a widow."[468] Curses were also bound with oaths in the ancient Mediterranean, which remains true even to this day, with traditions such as swearing on the Bible.[469]

The use of *defixiones* died out in antiquity, but their usefulness to scholars

---

[465] Bryan Ward-Perkins, *The Fall of Rome and the End of Civilization* (Oxford: Oxford University Press, 2005), 117ff. describes the disappearance of not only Roman rule, but the basic skills essential to Romano-British life.

[466] Leslie F. Smith, "A Pagan Parallel to 'Curse of Ernulphus,'" *The Classical Journal* 46, no. 6 (1951): 303-304.

[467] Lester K. Little, *Benedictine Maledictions: Liturgical Cursing in Romanesque France* (Ithaca, NY: Cornell University Press, 1993), 154.

[468] Little, *Benedictine Maledictions*, 126. Original Latin: "*Fiant dies eius pauci et fiant filii eius orphani et uxor eius vidua.*"

[469] David Martinez, "'May She Neither Eat Nor Drink': Love Magic and Vows of Abstinence," in *Ancient Magic and Ritual Power*, ed. Marvin Meyer and Paul Mirecki (Boston: Brill Academic Publishers, 2001), 344-45.

remains. The Romano-British curse tablets show how the world view of the Britons did not drastically change during the centuries of Roman rule, despite the superficial changes to their religion and society. The Britons may have become economically integrated with the Empire, the names of their gods may have changed, and their own names may have changed, but the Britons refused to give up their native culture.

Appendix: The Curse Tablets

Notes on the Curse Tablets

Both text and translations have been simplified. Latin texts are shown reconstructed or transported where needed, and include inserted letters where they are missing due to illegibility, missing section, or misspelling. As in all reconstructions, their accuracy is not assured, although many are almost certain due to conventions in curse tablet formulas. Most of the translated texts are an amalgam of expert translations, i.e. Tomlin, Collingwood, and my own interpretation. Translations that I had no hand in are noted. Tablets that consisted of only names were not translated.

Artifacts that are possibly curse tablets, but are not recognized by other authors as being curse tablets are referred to as possible curse tablet. The information from these is included in the statistics. Not all curse tablets found in Britain are in this database. Those excluded are extremely fragmentary and unable to aid in the understanding of Roman-Britain and the mechanisms of curse tablets. A couple of the fragmentary curse tablets are included for demonstration purposes.

Unless noted, tablets were not found in a folded state. However, since most of the tablets were found in a fragmented form, they may have been folded without knowledge of the archeologists who discovered them. Similarly, missing pieces of curse tablets may have been pierced by nails.

Alcester
1. Marius
Original: "Mariv" Reverse: c6CEc4"
Translation: "Marius"
Size: 90 x 15mm; Material: Lead strip; Holes/Nails: Neither; Location/ Date Found: 1983 under Stratford House; Deities: None; Names: Marius; Reason for Curse: Unknown; Other: Folded several times. [470]

Bath
2. Theft of Vilbia
Transpositioned Latin Version: "qu[i] mihi Vilviam in[v]olavit / sic liquat co[odo] aqua / . . . qui eam [invol]avit / Velvinna Ex[s]upereus / Verianus Serverinus / Agustalis Comitianus / Minianus Catus / Germanill[a] Iovina."

---

[470] Collingwood, *Roman Inscriptions of Britain* I #2436.5.

Translation: "May he who carried off Vilbia from me become as liquid as water . . . who stolen her, whether Velvinna, Exsupereus, Severinus, Augustalis, Comitianus, Minianus, Catus, Germanilla, Jovina."
Size: 68 x 68mm; Material: Sheet of alloyed metal; Holes/Nails: Neither; Location/ Date Found: 1880 in spring under the King's Bath; Deities: None; Names: Velvinna, Exsupereus, Severinus, Augustalis, Comitianus, Minianus, Catus, Germanilla, Jovina ; Reason for Curse: Kidnapping or elopement; Other: Words written in reverse, but in correct word order, [471] recent research has shown that Vilbia was a girl's name.[472]

3. List of Names
Original: "Severianus fil[ius] Brigomall[a]e / Patarnianus filius / Matarunus ussor / Catonius Potentini / Marinianus Belcati / Lucillus Lucciani / Aeternus Ingenui / Bellaus Bellini"
Translation: "Serverianus son of Brigomalla, Patarnianus her son, Matarnus his wife, Catonius son of Potentinus, Marinianus son of Belcatus, Lucillus son of Luccianus, Aeternus son of Ingenuus, Ballaus son of Bellinus"
Size: 145mm in diameter; Material: Pewter; Holes/Nails: Neither; Location/ Date Found: 1980 in spring under the King's Bath; Deities: None; Names: Serverianus, Brigomalla, Patarnianus, Matarnus, Catonius, Potentinus, Marinianus, Belcatus, Lucillus, Luccianus, Aeternus, Ingenuus, Ballaus, Bellinus; Reason for Curse: Unknown; Other: Folded twice.[473]

4. Six *Argentei*
Transpositioned Latin Version: "seu gen[tilli]s seu C / h[r]istianus quaecumque utrum vir / utrum mulier utrum puer utrum puella / utrum servus utrum liber mihi Annian / o mantutene de bursa mea s[e]x argente[o]s / furaverit tu d[o]mina dea ab ipso perxi[g] / e [eo]s si mihi per [f]raudem aliquam INDEP / REGSTVM dederit nec sic ipsi dona sed ut sangu / inem suum EPVTES qui mihi hoc inrogaverit" Transposition Reverse: "Postum[ianu]s Pisso / Locinna Alauna / Meterna Gunsula / C[an]didina Euticius / Peregrinus / Latinus / Senicianus / Avitanus / Victor / Scu[tri]us / Aessicunia / Paltucca / Calliopis / Celerianus"

[471] Collingwood, *Roman Inscriptions of Britain* I #154.

[472] L. J. F Keppie, A. S. Esmonde Cleary, M. W. C. Hassall, R. S. O. Tomlin, and Barry C. Burnham "Roman Britain in 1998," *Britannia* 30 (1999): 381.

[473] Collingwood, *Roman Inscriptions of Britain* I #2417.9.

Translation: "Whether pagan or Christian, whoever it is, whether man or woman, boy or girl, slave or free has stolen from me, Annianus, if Matutina, [has taken] six argentei from my purse, you, lady goddess, exact them from him. If through some deceit he has give me . . . and do not thus give to him but . . . his blood who has invoked this on me . . ."
Size: 105 x 60mm; Material: Sheet of lead; Holes/Nails: Neither; Location/ Date Found: 1979 in spring under King's Bath; Deities: Not given, but suggests Sulis-Minerva; Names: Annianus, Postumianus, Pisso, Locinna, Alauna, Materna, Gunsula, Candidina, Euticius, Peregrinus, Latinus, Senicianus, Avitinus, Victor, Seutrius, Aessicunia, Paltucca, Calliopis, Celerianus; Reason for Curse: Theft of six silver pieces. Other: Perhaps one of the most difficult curse tablets to decipher, the words were written from left the right, the lines were written in reverse order, and there are numerous mistakes.[474]

5. Six Silver Pieces
Original: "[D]eae Suli donavi . . . [arg]/[e]ntiolos sex quos perd[idi] / a nomin[i]bus infrascript[is] / deae exactura est / Senicianus et Saturniinus sed / et Ann[i]ola carta picta perscri[pta]" Reverse: "An[i]ola / Senicianus / Saturnius"
Translation: "I have given to the goddess Sulis the six silver pieces which I have lost. It is for the goddess to exact it from the debtors written below: Senicianus and Saturninus and Anniola. The draft has been copied."
Size: 95 x 54mm; Material: Sheet of tin/lead alloy; Holes/Nails: One possible nail hole; Location/ Date Found: 1979 in reservoir under the King's Bath; Deities: Sulis; Names: Senicianus, Saturninus, and Anniola; Reason for Curse: Theft of six silver pieces.[475]

6. Eleven Names
Original: "Severa / Draconitus / Spectatus / Innocentius / Senicio / Candidianus / [Si]mplicius / Belator / Surilla / Austus / Carinianu[s]"
Size: 53 x 113mm; Material: Lead/tin alloy; Holes/Nails: Neither; Location/ Date Found: 1979 in reservoir under the King's Bath; Deities: None; Names: Severa, Dracontius, Spectatus, Innocentius, Senicio, Candidianus, Simplicius, Belator, Surilla, Augustus, Carinianus; Reason for Curse: Unknown. [476]

---

[474] N. B. Rankov, M. W. C. Hassall, and R. S. O. Tomlin, "Roman Britain in 1981," *Britannia* 13 (1981): 404-406.

[475] F. O. Grew, M. W. C. Hassall, and R. S. O. Tomlin, "Roman Britain in 1980," *Britannia* 12 (1981): 370-372.

7. Stolen Cloak
Original: "Docilianus / Bruceri [filius] / deae sanctissim[a]e / Suli / devoveo
eum [q]ui / caracellam mean / involaverit si / vir si femina si / servus si liber /
ut . . . us dea Sulis / maximo letum / [a]digat nec ei so/mnum permit"
Reverse/continued "tat nec natos nec / nascentes do/[ne]c caracallam / meam
ad tem/plum sui numi/nus per[t]ulerit"
Translation: "Docilianus son of Brucerus to the most holy goddess Sulis. I curse
him who has stolen my hooded cloak, whether man or woman, slave or free, that
. . . the goddess Sulis inflicts death upon . . . not allow him sleep or children now
and in the future, until he has brought my cloak to the temple of her divinity."
Size: 70 x 100mm; Material: Sheet of lead/tin alloy; Holes/Nails: Neither;
Location/ Date Found: 1979 in reservoir under King's Bath; Deities: Sulis;
Names: Docilianus, Brucerus; Reason for Curse: Theft of a cloak. [477]

8. Perjury
Original: "Uricalus Do[c]ilosa uxor sua / Docilis filius suus et Docilina /
Dencentinus frater suus Alogiosa / nomina eorum qui iuraverunt / qui
iuraverunt ad fontem deae Suli[s] / prid[i]e idus Apriles quicumque illic
per/iuraverit deae Suli facias illum / sanguine suo illud satisfacere"
Translation: "Uricalus, Docilosa his wife, Docilis his son and Docilina, Decentius
his brother, Alogiosa: the names of those who have sworn at the spring of the
goddess Suils on the twelfth of April. Whosoever there has perjured himself you
are to make him pay for it to the goddess Sulis in his own blood."
Size: 75 x 55mm; Material: Cast sheet of tin/lead alloy; Holes/Nails: Neither;
Location/ Date Found: 1979 in spring under the King's Bath; Deities: Sulis;
Names: Uricalus, Docilosa, Docilis, Docilina, Decentinus, Algiosa; Reason for
Curse: A curse for any of the named persons who committed perjury; Other:
Handwriting suggests third century.[478]

9. Three Names
Original: "Brittuenda / Marinus / Memorina"
Size: 75 x 75mm; Material: Sheet of lead/tin alloy; Holes/Nails: Neither;

---

[476] Grew, et al, "Roman Britain in 1980," 372-373

[477] Grew, et al, "Roman Britain in 1980," 372-377.

[478] Grew, et al, "Roman Britain in 1980," 375, 378.

Location/ Date Found: 1979 in the spring under the King's Bath; Deities: None; Names: Brittudenda, Marinus, Memorina; Reason for Curse: Unknown; Other: Had been folded.[479]

10. Theft
Original: "Nomen / furis qui / LATERA" Reverse: "IRQVET / donatu/r . . ."
Translation: "The name of the thief who . . . " Reverse: " . . . is given . . ."
Size: 77 x57mm; Material: Lead/tin alloy sheet; Holes/Nails: Two nail holes; Location/ Date Found: 1979 in the spring under the King's Bath; Deities: None; Names: None; Reason for Curse: Theft, non-specific.[480]

11. Victory and the Tax Collector
Original: "Pet[it]io / rove te / Victoria vind . . . /cun . . . Minici / Cunomolius / Minervina ussor / Cunitius ser[v]us / Senovara ussor / Lavidendus ser[v]us / Mattonius ser[v]us / Catinius exsactoris / furem / Methianu[s] . . ." Reverse: " . . . [a]micus . . . / TPIASV / GINENINVSV[S] / gienunus" Detached fragment: ". . . dono"
Translation: "The petition . . . Victory . . . Cunommolius son of Minicus, and Minervina his wise, Cunitius the slave and Senovara his wife, Lavidendus the slave, Mattonius the slave, Catinius the tax collector's thief, Methianus" Reverse: ". . . a friends . . . Iginunus" Detached fragment: "I give. . ."
Size: 60 x 90mm; Material: Tin/lead alloy sheet; Holes/Nails: Neither; Location/ Date Found: 1979 in the spring under the King's Bath; Deities: None; Names: Victoria, Vindocunus, Cunomolius, Minervina, Cunitius, Senovara, Lavidendus, Mattonius, Catinius, Methianus, Igienunus; Reason for Curse: Unknown; Other: Tablet had been rolled up, the two sides were written by different hands.[481]

12. Stolen Bracelet
Original: "nomen rei / qui destra / le involave / rit"
Translation: "The name of the culprit who has stolen my bracelet"
Size: 63 x 63mm; Material: Sheet of lead; Holes/Nails: Neither; Location/ Date Found: 1979 in spring under King's Bath; Deities: None; Names: None; Reason for Curse: Theft of a bracelet. [482]

---

[479] Rankov, et al, "Roman Britain in 1981," 397-398.

[480] Rankov, et al, "Roman Britain in 1981," 398-399.

[481] Rankov, et al, "Roman Britain in 1981," 398, 400.

[482] Rankov, et al, :Roman Britain in 1981," 401-402.

13. Five *Denarii*

Original: "Deae Suli Minervae Docca / dono numini tuo pecuniam quam / misi id est [denarios quinque] et is [q]ui / . . . [eam involaveri]t si ser[vu]s s[i liber] . . . / . . . ex s igatur . . ."

Translation: "To the goddess Sulis Minerva from Docca. I give to your divinity the money which I have lost by theft, this is, five *denarii*, and he who has stolen it, whether slave or free . . . is to be compelled . . ."

Size: 98 x 66mm; Material: Tin/lead alloy sheet; Holes/Nails: One nail hole; Location/ Date Found: 1979 in the spring under the King's Bath; Deities: Sulis Minerva; Names: Docca; Reason for Curse: Theft of five *denarii*.[483]

14. Mars and the Silver Ring

Original: "Basilia donat in templum Martis ani/lum argentuem si servus si liber [ta]/ m[e]dius fuerit vel aliquid de hoc / noverit ut sanguin[e] et liminibus ob"

Reverse: "omnibus membris configatur vel et/iam intestinis excomesis [om]nibus habet[at] / is qui anilum involavit vet qui medius / fuerit" On first side, perpendicular to other writing: "Primurudem"

Translation: "Basilia gives to the temple of Mars her silver ring, and asks that so long as someone whether slave or free have been privy to or knows anything about it he may be cursed in his blood and eyes and" Reverse: "every limb, or even have all his intestines eaten away if he has stolen the ring or been privy to it."

Size: 128 x 49mm; Material: Tin/lead alloy sheet; Holes/Nails: Neither; Location/ Date Found: 1979 in spring under King's Bath; Deities: Mars; Names: Basilia, Primurudem; Reason for Curse: Theft of a silver ring.[484]

15. Eight Names

Original: "Cunsa / Docimedis / Sedebelia / Maria / Vendibedis / Cunsus / Severiaanus / Seniila"

Size: 59 x 22mm; Material: Lead/tin alloy casting; Holes/Nails: Neither; Location/ Date Found: 1979 in spring under King's Bath; Deities: None; Names: Cunsa, Docimedis, Sedebelia, Maria, Vendibedis, Cunsus, Severianus, Senila; Reason for Curse: Unknown; Other: Handwriting suggests fourth century dating.[485]

---

[483] Rankov, et al, "Roman Britain in 1981," 401, 403, and 406.

[484] S. S. Frere, M W. C. Hassall, and R. S. O. Tomlin, "Roman Britain in 1982," *Britannia* 14 (1983): 336, 338, revisions in "Roman Britain in 1990," 308.

[485] Frere, et al, "Roman Britain in 1982," 336 and 339.

16. Seven Names
Original: "Victorinus / Talipieinus / Minatius / Victorianus / Campe/pedita / Valauneicus / aBelia"
Size: 58 x 22mm; Material: Casting of lead/tin alloy; Holes/Nails: Neither; Location/ Date Found: 1979 in spring under King's Bath; Deities: None; Names: Victorinus, Talipieinus, Minatius, Victorianus, Campedita, Valauneicus, Belia; Reason for Curse: Unknown; Other: Appears to be in the same hand as tablet above. [486]

17. Deomiorix's Robbed House
Original: "Execro qui involaver/it qui Deomiorix de hos/ipitio suo perdiderit qui/cumque re[u]s deus illum / inveniat sanguine et / vitae suae illud redemat"
Translation: "I curse him who has stolen, who has robbed Deomiorix from his house. Whosoever guilty to the god finds him, let him recover it with blood and his life."
Size: 75 x 39mm; Material: Sheet of tin; Holes/Nails: Neither; Location/ Date Found: 1979 in spring under King's Bath; Deities: None; Names: Deomiorix; Reason for Curse: Theft; Other: Handwriting suggests fourth century dating, second line was written backwards. [487]

18. Stolen *Caracalla*
Original: "Minervae / de[ae] Suli donavi / furem qui / caracallam / mean invo/lavit si servus / si liber si ba/ro si mulier / hoc donum non / redemat nessi / sangu[i]ne suo"
Translation: "I have given to the goddess Minerva Sulis the thief who has stolen my hooded cloak, whether slave or free, whether man or woman. He is not the recover this gift unless with his own blood."
Size: 49 x 88 mm; Material: Tin/lead alloy; Holes/Nails: Neither; Location/ Date Found: 1979 in spring under King's Bath; Deities: Sulis Minerva; Names: None; Reason for Curse: Theft of a hooded cloak. [488]

19. Theft of a Bronze Vessel
Transpositioned Latin Version: "a[e]n[um me]um qui levavit [e]xc/onic[tu]s [e]st temlo Sulis / dono si mulier si baro si ser/vus si liber si pure si puella / et qui

---

[486] Frere, et al, "Roman Britain in 1982," 336-337, and 341.

[487] Frere, et al, "Roman Britain in 1982," 336 and 339.

[488] Frere, et al, "Roman Britain in 1982," 336 and 340.

hoc fecerit san/gu[in]em suum in ipsum aen/mu fundat" Reverse: "dono si mul[ie]r si / ba[ro] si servus si lib/er si puer puel/la eum latr[on]/em qui rem ipsa/m involavi[t] d/eus [i]nvenia[t]"
Translation: "The person who has lifted my bronze vessel is utterly accursed. I give him to the temple of Sulis, whether man or woman, whether slave or free, whether boy or girl, and let him who has done this spill his own blood into the vessel itself." Reverse: "I give, whether woman or man, whether slave or free, whether boy or girl, that thief who has stolen the property itself that they god may find him."
Size: 75 x 58mm; Material: Tin/lead alloy sheet; Holes/Nails: Neither; Location/ Date Found: 1979 in the spring under the King's Bath; Deities: None; Names: None; Reason for Curse: Theft of a bronze vessel; Other: Tablet had been folded twice, poorly spelled.[489]

20. Two Names
Original: "Britivenda / Venibelia"
Size: 60 x 37mm; Material: Tin/lead alloy sheet; Holes/Nails: Neither; Location/ Date Found: 1979 in spring under King's Bath; Deities: None; Names: Britivenda, Venibelia; Reason for Curse: Unknown. [490]

21. Lovernisca's Plea
Transpositioned Latin Version: "Lovernisca d[onat] / eum qui sive v[ir] / isive femina s[i]ve / puer sive puella / qui ina . . sortium . i[n]volaverit"
Translation: "Lovernisca gives him who, whether man or woman, whether boy or girl, who has stolen . . ."
Size: 55 x 46mm; Material: Lead/tin alloy sheet; Holes/Nails: One nail hole; Location/ Date Found: 1979 in spring under King's Bath; Deities: None; Names: Lovernisca; Reason for Curse: Theft; Other: Letters written in reverse order. [491]

22. Typical Theft Formula
Original: ". . . [perm]ittas / . . . [somn]um nec sanita/[tem . . . n]isi tandiu ta/ . . . iat quandiu hoc / . . . [ill]ud se habuerit / . . . si vir si femina et / . . . si ancilla"
Translation: ". . . you are not to permit . . . sleep or health . . . except for as long as . . . he shall be . . . whether man or woman and . . . or slave girl."

[489] S. S. Frere, M W. C. Hassall, and R. S. O. Tomlin, "Roman Britain in 1983," *Britannia* 15 (1984):333-335.

[490] Frere, et al, "Roman Britain in 1983," 333 and 336.

[491] Frere, et al, "Roman Britain in 1983," 333 and 337.

Size: 61 x 72mm; Material: Tin/lead alloy sheet; Holes/Nails: Neither; Location/ Date Found: 1979 in spring under King's Bath; Deities: None; Names: None; Reason for Curse: not given, but remnants suggest it was theft. [492]

23. Stolen Gloves

Original: "Docimedis / [p]erdidit[t] mani/cilla dua qui / illas involavi[t] / ut mentes sua[s] / perd[at] et / oculos su[o]s / in fano ubi / destina[t]"
Translation: "Docimedis has lost two gloves. He asks that the person who has stolen them should lose his mind and his eyes in the temple where she appoints."
Size: 68 x 99 mm; Material: Lead/tin alloy sheet; Holes/Nails: Neither; Location/ Date Found: 1979 in spring under King's Bath; Deities: None; Names: Docimedis; Reason for Curse: Theft of a pair of gloves. [493]

24. Stolen Clothing

Original: ". . . eocrotis perdedi la[enam] / [pa]lleum sagum paxsam do[navi] / . . . [S]ulis ut hoc ant dies novem / [si li]ber si ser[v]us si [li]bera si serva / [si] pu[er] si puell[a i]n rostr[o] s[uo] / defera[t] . . ./ caballarem s[i servus si liber si] / serva si libera si puer [si puella] / in suo rostro defer[at]"
Translation: "I . . . eocorotis have lost my cloak and tunic, I have given . . . Sulis that he may bring it down in the snout before nine days, whether free or slave, whether free woman or slave woman, whether boy or girl . . . horse blanket . . . whether slave or free, whether slave woman or free woman, whether boy or girl, bring down in his snout."
Size: 65 x 56mm; Material: Lead/tin alloy sheet; Holes/Nails: Neither; Location/ Date Found: 1980 in the spring under the King's Bath; Deities: Sulis; Names: . . . eocorotis; Reason for Curse: Theft of a cloak and tunic. [494]

25. Theft of a Rug

Original: "stragulum q[ue]m / [p]erdid anim[a]. . . [invo]/lavit . . .nisi / s[an]g[u]ine sua."
Translation: ". . . the rug which I have lost . . . his life . . . has stolen . . . unless with his own blood."

---

[492] Frere, et al, "Roman Britain in 1983," 336 and 338 and Tomlin, "The Curse Tablets," 178, no. 52.

[493] S. S. Frere, M W. C. Hassall, and R. S. O. Tomlin, "Roman Britain in 1985," *Britannia* 17 (1986): 430 and 432.

[494] S. S. Frere, M W. C. Hassall, and R. S. O. Tomlin, "Roman Britain in 1986," *Britannia* 18 (1987): 364.

Size: 60 x 62mm; Material: Lead alloy sheet; Holes/Nails: Neither; Location/
Date Found: In the spring under the King's Bath; Deities: None; Names: None;
Reason for Curse: Theft of a rug or blanket; Other: folded once. [495]

26. Bloody Fragment
Original: "...[s]/ang[ine] / noctis / qui mih[i] / uui..."
Translation: "...blood...night...what I..."
Size: 26 x 33mm; Material: 'Brassy' metal of unknown composition; Holes/Nails:
Neither; Location/ Date Found: In the spring under the King's Bath; Deities:
None; Names: None; Reason for Curse: Unknown[496]

27. Fragment
Original: "... [invo]/laver[it] ... / furerit .../vi si l[iber si servus quicum]/que
co ..."
Translation: "...sieze upon ... the theif ... whether free or slave and who ..."
Size: 25 x 32mm; Material: Lead alloy sheet; Holes/Nails: Neither; Location/
Date Found: In the spring under King's Bath; Deities: None; Names: None;
Reason for Curse: Theft.[497]

28. Fragment
Original: "... ve... /... diabt .../ [si l]iber [si servus] ..."
Translation: "... whether free or slave ..."
Size: 17 x 32mm; Material: Lead alloy sheet; Holes/Nails: Neither; Location/
Date Found: In the spring under King's Bath; Deities: None; Names: None;
Reason for Curse: Unknown.[498]

29. Garbled Fragment
Original: "... marin[us].../... quas pe[rdidi] / ... tiolo meo .. / [i]nvolaverit si
..."
Translation: "... who destroys ... my ... seize ..."
Size: 28 x 23mm; Material: Unknown; Holes/Nails: Neither; Location/ Date
Found: In the spring under King's Bath; Deities: None; Names: None; Reason for
Curse: Unknown.[499]

---

[495] Tomlin, "The Curse Tablets," 116, no. 6.

[496] Tomlin, "The Curse Tablets," 117, no. 7.

[497] Tomlin, "The Curse Tablets," 124, no.11a.

[498] Tomlin, "The Curse Tablets," 124 no.11b.

[499] Tomlin, "The Curse Tablets," 125 no.12a.

30. Fragment

Original: ". . . involaverit . . .llum invola/[verit] . . . virus . . . mulieris . . . illido . . .us / . . . . llum vitali . . ./espeditus. . . tatirum . . ."

Translation: ". . . seize . . . those things . . . woman . . . striking . . . vital . . . obtain . . ."

Size: 85 x 52mm; Material: Sheet of lead; Holes/Nails: Neither; Location/ Date Found: In the spring under King's Bath; Deities: None; Names: Vitalis, Expeditus, Tatrim; Reason for Curse: Unknown.[500]

31. Celtic Tablet

Original: "luciumio / cittimediu . . .xs / uibec . . .traceos / estaidimaui . . . / itttlemmancatacimluci / lendiierandant . . . nn . . . / uc . . .miotouesulara . . . irando . . / . . . mnottanoumdii / . . . cii . . . eleubarrau . . . / . . . staginemse . . . / . . . fer . . . / . . . r. . ."

Translation: ". . . storehouse . . . /. . . stole from me, a son of the fosterage of Cimluci. . . / . . . You make claim upon . . ."

Size: 56 x 40mm; Material: Alloy sheet; Holes/Nails: Neither; Location/ Date Found: In the spring under King's Bath; Deities: None; Names: Cimluci; Reason for Curse: Theft; Other: It is the opinion of Tomlin, the foremost scholar on Romano-British inscriptions, that the language written is in fact Celtic. Only a couple of lines can be read, but it is clearly ancient British Celtic and the discernable words are similar to other curse tablets. This is a remarkable lead tablet, since it is one of the earliest examples of written Celtic, and it is proof that the idea of curse tablets was adopted by the local population.[501]

32. Six Names

Original: "Senianus / Magnus / Mc. . ." Reverse: "Lucianu[s] Marcellianus / [M]allainus / Mu[t]ata Medol. . ./ geacus."

Size: 69 x 23mm; Material: Tin alloy blob; Holes/Nails: Neither; Location/ Date Found: In the spring under King's Bath; Deities: None; Names: Senianus, Magnus, Lucianus, Marcellianus, Mallainus, Mutata; Reason for Curse: Unknown. [502]

---

[500] Tomlin, "The Curse Tablets," 127, no. 13.

[501] Tomlin, "The Curse Tablets," 128 no. 14. Translation from Celtic by Mark Bradley.

[502] Tomlin, "The Curse Tablets," 132, no. 17.

33. Celtic Names
Original: "Adixoui / deiana / deieda / andagin / uindiorix / cuamiin / ai"
Size: 35-38mm in diameter; Material: Probably tin; Holes/Nails: Neither;
Location/ Date Found: In the spring under King's Bath; Deities: None; Names:
Adixoui, Deiana, Deieda, Andagin, Uindiorix, Cuamiinai; Reason for Curse:
Unknown; Other: All names are Celtic. [503]

34. Plea to Sulis
Original: ". . . .em det nisi / . . . in vero d[e]ae S[ulis]. . . ."
Translation: ". . . unless . . . the goddess Sulis. . ."
Size: 36 x 21mm; Material: Unknown; Holes/Nails: Neither; Location/ Date
Found: In the spring under King's Bath; Deities: Sulis; Names: None; Reason for
Curse: Probably theft.[504]

35. Sulis
Original: ". . . [d]eae Su[li]. . . ."
Translation: ". . . goddess Sulis. . ."
Size: 39 x 19mm; Material: Unknown; Holes/Nails: Neither; Location/ Date
Found: In the spring under King's Bath; Deities: Sulis; Names: None; Reason for
Curse: Unknown.[505]

36. Dedication to Sulis
Original: ". . . [dea] Sulis t[ibi] . . ./ . . .en. . ."
Translation: ". . . to you, goddess Sulis. . ."
Size: 21 x 16mm; Material: Unknown; Holes/Nails: Neither; Location/ Date
Found: In the spring under King's Bath; Deities: Sulis; Names: None; Reason for
Curse: Probably theft. [506]

37. Stolen Ploughshare
Original: "si [qui]s vome/rem Civilis / involavit / ut an[imam] / suua[m] in
tem/plo deponat / [si n]o[n] vom/[erem] . . .ub/ . . .[si se]rvus / si liber si
li/bertinus . . ./ unan . . o / finem faci/[a]m"

---

[503] Tomlin, "The Curse Tablets," 133, no. 18.

[504] Tomlin, "The Curse Tablets," 134, no. 19.

[505] Tomlin, "The Curse Tablets," 135, no. 20a.

[506] Tomlin, "The Curse Tablets," 136, no. 21.

Translation: "If anyone has stolen Civilis' ploughshare I ask that he lay down his life in the temple unless . . . the ploughshare, whether slaver or free or freedman. . . I make an end to . . ."

Size: 36 x 88mm; Material: Alloy sheet; Holes/Nails: Neither; Location/ Date Found: In the spring under King's Bath; Deities: None; Names: Civilis; Reason for Curse: Theft of a ploughshare; Other: Folded thrice. [507]

38. Theft of a Tunic and Cloak

Original: " deae Suli Minerv[a]e Soli/nus dono numini tuo ma/iestati paxsa[m] ba[ln]earem et [pal]/leum [nec p]ermitta[s so]mnum / nec san[ita]tem ei qui mihi fr[a]u/dem [f]ecit si vir si femi[na] si servus / s[i] l[ib]er nissi [s]e retefens istas / s[p]ecies ad [te]mplum tuum detulerit / [li]beri sui vel son . . .sua e[t] qui / . . . deg . . ./ ei quoque . . . xe . . ./ . . . [so]mnum ne[c sanitate]/m . . .n . . .alul[e]um / et relinq[ua]s nissi ad [te]mplum tu/um istas res retulerint"

Translation: "Solinus to the goddess Sulis Minerva. I give to your divinity and majesty my bathing tunic and cloak. Do not allow sleep or health to him who has done me wrong, whether man or woman, whether slave or free, unless he reveals himself and brings those goods to your temple. . . his children or his . . .and who . . . to him also . . .sleep or health . . . cloak and the rest unless they bring those things to your temple."

Size: 78 x 91mm; Material: Alloy sheet; Holes/Nails: Neither; Location/ Date Found: In the spring under King's Bath; Deities: Sulis Minerva; Names: Solinus; Reason for Curse: Theft of cloak and bathing tunic; Other: Folded four times. [508]

39. Plea to Mars

Original: "deo Marti . . ./ do[no] maiest[ati tuo] / sacellum . . ./ nisi e . . ."

Translation: "To the god Mars. . . give to your majesty . . . shrine . . .unless. . ."

Size: 37 x 38mm; Material: Alloy sheet; Holes/Nails: Neither; Location/ Date Found: In the spring under King's Bath; Deities: Mars; Names: None; Reason for Curse: Theft. [509]

40. Vengeance

Original: "deae Sul[i] Minervae / rogo [s]anctissimam / maiestatem tuam u[t] / vindices ab his [q]ui [fra]/[ude]m fecerunt ut ei[s per]/mittas nec s[o]mnum [nec] . . . ."

[507] Tomlin, "The Curse Tablets," 148, no. 31.

[508] Tomlin, "The Curse Tablets," 150, no. 32.

[509] Tomlin, "The Curse Tablets," 152, no. 33.

Translation: "To the goddess Sulis Minerva, I ask your most sacred majesty that you take vengeance on those who have done me wrong, that you permit them neither sleep nor. ."
Size: 61 x 46mm; Material: Cast alloy sheet; Holes/Nails: Neither; Location/ Date Found: In the spring under King's Bath; Deities: Sulis Minerva; Names: None; Reason for Curse: Vengeance for unspecified crime.[510]

41. Theft
Original: ". . . q . . ./ et invol[vit] . . . / duo de. . ./ adhuisgar . . ./ deveniat si lib[er] / si ser[v]us si puer [si] / [p]uella si vir s[i]. . ."
Translation: ". . . and has stolen . . . two . . . whether free or slave, whether boy or girl, whether man or woman . . ."
Size: 59 x 55mm; Material: Alloy sheet; Holes/Nails: Neither; Location/ Date Found: In the spring under King's Bath; Deities: None; Names: None; Reason for Curse: Theft; Other: Folded. [511]

42. May Their Lives Be Weakened
Original: "illorum anima / las[s]er[ur] / titumus / sedileubisediac / uaquepanum" Reverse: "exsibuus / lothuius / mascntius / aesibuas / petiacus"
Translation: "May their life be weakened: Titumus, Sedileubus, Sediacus, Exsibuus, Lothuius, Masentius, Aesibuas, Petiacus."
Size: 68 x 48mm; Material: Alloy sheet; Holes/Nails: One nail hole; Location/ Date Found: In the spring under King's Bath; Deities: None; Names: Titumus, Sedileubus, Sediacus, Exsibuus, Lothuius, Masentius, Aesibuas, Petiacus; Reason for Curse: Vengeance.[512]

43. Revenge Against a Thief
Original: ". . . dono ti/[bi] . . . ream / . . .l . . . sivio meo / . . . [e]x[i]gas pe[r sa]/[nguinem e[ius] qui has / [involave]rit vel qui / [medius fuer]it si femina /. . . o [si] liber/ . . . sa . . ./ . . .um pertuleri[t]"
Translation: ". . . I give to you . . . that you may exact them through the blood of him who has stolen these or who has been privy to it, whether woman . . . whether free . . . has brought . . ."

[510] Tomlin, "The Curse Tablets," 154, no. 35.
[511] Tomlin, "The Curse Tablets," 155, no. 36.
[512] Tomlin, "The Curse Tablets," 156, no. 37.

Size: 46 x 75mm; Material: Alloy sheet; Holes/Nails: Neither; Location/ Date Found: In the spring under King's Bath; Deities: None; Names: None; Reason for Curse: Theft; Other: Folded four times. [513]

44. Totia
Original: "qui involaverit / si ser[v]us si lib[e]r / . . . ./ Totia / anima[m] suam / [q]u[i i]nvolav . . / . . . a[m] meam / . . . / qu[i] in/volavi . . ."
Translation: "Who has stolen, whether slave or free. . . .Totia . . . his life . . . who has stolen . . . my . . . who has stolen . . ."
Size: 91 x 48mm; Material: Alloy blob; Holes/Nails: Neither; Location/ Date Found: In the spring under King's Bath; Deities: None; Names: Totia; Reason for Curse: Theft; Other: Folded four times. [514]

45. False Accusations
Original: "qui alamaea / negat sanguine / . . . inen . . . / de[s]t[in]at"
Translation: "Let him who denies making false accusation . . . blood . . . she appoints."
Size: 92 x 58mm; Material: Alloy sheet; Holes/Nails: Neither; Location/ Date Found: In the spring under King's Bath; Deities: None; Names: None; Reason for Curse: False accusations. [515]

46. The Price of Theft
Original: ". . . [r]ipuit ut [eo]rum pretium / . . .[et e]xigas hoc per sanguinem et sa/[nitatem sua]m et suorm nec ante illos pati[a]r/[is bibere nec m]manducare nec adsellare nec / . . . ius hoc . . .bisoverit."
Translation: ". . . has stolen that . . . the price of them and exact this through his blood and health and those of his family, and not allow them to drink or eat or defecate or urinate before he as . . . this."
Size: 108 x 44 mm; Material: Tin alloy sheet; Holes/Nails: Neither; Location/ Date Found: In the spring under King's Bath; Deities: None; Names: None; Reason for Curse: Theft; Other: Folded. [516]

47. Theft of a Cloak
Original: ". . . pu / . . . dono ti[bi] / [p]alliu[m]. . ."

---

[513] Tomlin, "The Curse Tablets," 157, no. 38.

[514] Tomlin, "The Curse Tablets," 158, no. 39.

[515] Tomlin, "The Curse Tablets," 159, no. 40.

[516] Tomlin, "The Curse Tablets," 160 no. 41.

Translation: "... I give to you ... cloak..."
Size: 27 x 29mm; Material: Tin alloy; Holes/Nails: Neither; Location/ Date
Found: In the spring under King's Bath; Deities: None; Names: None; Reason for
Curse: Theft of a cloak. [517]

48. Sulis

Original: "deae Suli ... / ... / ... is qu[i]" Reverse: "si servus si liber si quis
cumq[ue] / erit non illi permittas nec / oculos nec anitatem nisi caeciatatem /
orbitatemque quoad vixerit / nisi haec ad fanum ..."
Translation: "To the goddess Sulis .... whether slave or free, whoever he shall
be, you are not to permit him eyes or health unless blindness and childlessness
so long as he shall live, unless .... these to the temple."
Size: 64 x 41mm; Material: Alloy sheet; Holes/Nails: Neither; Location/ Date
Found: In the spring under King's Bath; Deities: Sulis; Names: None; Reason for
Curse: Theft; Other: Folded once. [518]

49. Sulis Minerva

Original: "desulimine... / aeeosquiamaliama ... / tlrasuendetsilumla .../
corregenetc .. egeet ... fan ... / tlsuu dea ... tedo ..../ etqohabunit ..
setrodeam / etsanuenesua ...bitquime / uitisetmalu .. ic...em/
docigeniusuteane..."
Translation: "To the goddess Sulis Minerva ..."
Size: 81 x 111mm; Material: Alloy sheet; Holes/Nails: None; Location/ Date
Found: In the spring under King's Bath; Deities: Sulis Minerva; Names: None;
Reason for Curse: Unknown; Other: Folded six times, too fragmented and
garbled to decode. [519]

50. Theft

Original: "...[tib]i q[u]er[or] / ... exxigi / [si servu]s si liber hoc tulerit / [non
il]li permittas in angu[i]ne / ...sui ..."
Translation: "... I complain to you ... be exacted... whether slave or free, has
taken this ...you are not to permit him in blood...his..."
Size: 66 x 36mm; Material: Lead; Holes/Nails: Neither; Location/ Date Found: In
the spring under King's Bath; Deities: None; Names: None; Reason for Curse:
Theft; Other: Folded twice. [520]

---

[517] Tomlin, "The Curse Tablets," 163 no. 43.

[518] Tomlin, "The Curse Tablets," 166 no. 45.

[519] Tomlin, "The Curse Tablets," 168 no. 46.

51. Horse Blanket

Original: "qu[i involvavi]t cab[al]/lar[e]m si [vir si f[emin[a] / si ser[v]us [si libe]r / . . .dea sul[is]. . ."

Translation: "The person who has stolen my horse blanket, whether man or woman, whether slave or free . . . goddess Sulis. . ."

Size: 33x 33mm and 16 x 30mm; Material: Unknown; Holes/Nails: Neither; Location/ Date Found: In the spring under King's Bath; Deities: Sulis; Names: None; Reason for Curse: Theft of a horse blanket; Other: Consists of two conjoining fragments. [521]

52. The Cursing of Families

Original: "d[eo] Mercurio / . . [C]ivilis . . . fuerit de / . . Trinni familiam . . ./ Velvalis . . ./ am suam." Reverse: "Markelinum familia[m] /Velorigam et famili[am] / [s]uam Morivassum et / [f]amiliam Riovassum e[t] / familiam Minoven . . /et familiam sua[m]. ."

Translation: "To the god Mercury. . . Civilis . . . shall have been . . . family of Trinnus . . . his. . . Marcellinus and his family, Velorga and her family, Morvassus and his family, Riovassus and his family, Minover and his family. . ."

Size: 65 x 49mm; Material: Tin/lead alloy sheet; Holes/Nails: One nail hole; Location/ Date Found: In the spring under King's Bath; Deities: Mercury; Names: Civilis, Trinnus, Marcellinus, Velorga, Marivassus, Riovassus, Minoven; Reason for Curse: Unknown.[522]

53. Fragment

Original: ". . . / recentis. . .imi . . . / capitularem civi[lis] . . . / em supplic . . ./ si ser[vus si liber] . . . / somnus . . ."

Translation: ". . . recent . . . taxing of the city . . . whether slave or free. . ."

Size: 31 x 63mm; Material: Tin/lead alloy sheet; Holes/Nails: Neither; Location/ Date Found: In the spring under the King's Bath; Deities: None; Names: Civilis; Reason for Curse: Unknown.[523]

54. Exsibuus's Plea

Original: "deae . . . Exsib[uus] / dona[vit] i[l]los qui . . .ban/ . . .sunt . . . [si

---

[520] Tomlin, "The Curse Tablets," 170, no.47.

[521] Tomlin, "The Curse Tablets," 172 no. 49.

[522] Tomlin, "The Curse Tablets," 180 no. 53.

[523] Tomlin, "The Curse Tablets," 185 no. 55.

sercus] / si l[iber si bar]o si m[u]l[i]e[r]/ sa. . . ."
Translation: "To the goddess. . . Exsibuus has given those who . . . are . . .
whether slave or free, whether man or woman. . ."
Size: 66 x 51mm; Material: Lead/tin alloy sheet; Holes/Nails: Neither; Location/
Date Found: In the spring under the King's Bath; Deities: None; Names:
Exsibuus; Reason for Curse: Theft; Other: Folded several times. [524]

55. Enica
Original: "Enica conqueror ti[bi] / . . . tanulis . . . dehi . . ."
Translation: "I, Enica, complain to you . . ."
Size: 81 x 36mm; Material: Lead/tin alloy sheet; Holes/Nails: Neither; Location/
Date Found: In the spring under the King's Bath; Deities: None; Names: Enica;
Reason for Curse: Justice. [525]

56. Stolen Pan
Original: "Oconea deae Suli / M[inervae] dono [ti]bi pa/nnum si quis eum . . ."
Translation: "Oconea to the goddess Sulis Minerva, I give you a pan if anyone
has stolen it . . ."
Size: 59 x 29mm; Material: Lead/tin alloy sheet; Holes/Nails: Neither; Location/
Date Found: In the spring under the King's Bath; Deities: Sulis Minerva; Names:
Oconea; Reason for Curse: Theft of a pan. [526]

57. Theft of a Bathing Tunic
Original: "deae Suli / si quis balniarem / Cantissen[a]e inv[o]la[v]erit / si
s[e]r[v]u si liber . . ."
Translation: "To the goddess Sulis, if anyone has stolen the bathing tunic of
Cantissena, whether slave or free. . ."
Size: 83 x 50mm; Material: Lead blob; Holes/Nails: Neither; Location/ Date
Found: In the spring under the King's Bath; Deities: Sulis; Names: Cantissena;
Reason for Curse: Theft of a bathing tunic; Other: Folded. [527]

58. Stolen Cloak
Original: ". . . quiescit . . . lit sanitatem invictus / nisi eidem loco ipsum pallium /
[re]ducat"

---

[524] Tomlin, "The Curse Tablets," 187, no. 57.

[525] Tomlin, "The Curse Tablets," 190, no. 59.

[526] Tomlin, "The Curse Tablets," 191, no. 60.

[527] Tomlin, "The Curse Tablets," 196, no. 63.

Translation: "... rests ... health unconquered unless he brings the cloak itself back to the same place."
Size: 98 x 53mm; Material: Tin/lead alloy sheet; Holes/Nails: Neither, but appeared to be pierced with a knife; Location/ Date Found: In the spring under the King's Bath; Deities: None; Names: None; Reason for Curse: Theft of a cloak; Other: Folded five times. [528]

59. Theft of a Pan
Original: "exsuperius / donat pannum ferri / qui illi innoc[entiam] ...nfam / tusc ....su/ lis si vir [si femin]a s[i] ser[v]us / si liber ho[c] / ill ... / et ...er.../ suas inv[o]la[veru]n[t] s[i] vir / si femina s[ati]sfecerit / sanguin[e] ill[o]rum hoc / devindices [si] q[u]is aenum mi/hi involav[i]t"
Translation: "Exsuprius gives an iron pan ... who ... innocence fore him ... of Sulis, whether man or woman . ..whether slave or free ... this ... and ... have stolen his ... whether man or woman is to have given satisfaction with their blood. You are to reclaim this is anyone has stolen the vessel from me."
Size: 99 x 134mm; Material: Tin/lead alloy sheet; Holes/Nails: Neither; Location/ Date Found: In the spring under the King's Bath; Deities: Sulis; Names: Exsuperius; Reason for Curse: Theft of a pan; Other: Folded nine times. [529]

60. To Sulis
Original: "... ia ... / ... dea Suli[s] ... / ... nem d ..."
Translation "... the goddess Sulis ..."
Size: 24 x 27mm; Material: Unknown; Holes/Nails: Neither; Location/ Date Found: In the spring under the King's Bath; Deities: Sulis; Names: None; Reason for Curse: Unknown. [530]

61. Minerva
Original: "Minerv[a] ... / amcocus .../ lumpell..."
Size: 29 x 22mm; Material: Unknown; Holes/Nails: Neither; Location/ Date Found: In the spring under the King's Bath; Deities: Minerva; Names: None; Reason for Curse: Unknown. [531]

---

[528] Tomlin, "The Curse Tablets," 197, no. 64.

[529] Tomlin, "The Curse Tablets," 200, no. 66.

[530] Tomlin, "The Curse Tablets," 204, no. 69.

[531] Tomlin, "The Curse Tablets," 205, no. 70.

62. Theft

Original: ". . . qui suib . . . / [s]i se[rv]us s[i] . . ./ . . . si vir si [f]em[ina] . . . discebit . . ."

Translation: ". . . whether slave or free . . . whether man or woman . . . will learn . . ."

Size: 80 x 64mm; Material: Lead sheet; Holes/Nails: Neither; Location/ Date Found: In the spring under the King's Bath; Deities: None; Names: None; Reason for Curse: Most likely theft; Other: Folded.[532]

63. Bitilus Linus

Original: ". . .[B]itilus Linu[s] . . ./ . . .Bitiluus Lin[us] . . ."

Size: 53 x 67 mm; Material: Sheet of lead; Holes/Nails: Neither; Location/ Date Found: In the spring under the King's Bath; Deities: None; Names: Bitilus, Linus; Reason for Curse: Unknown; Other: Folded. [533]

64. Bushel of Smoke

Original: "si puer si puella / si vir si femina qui h[oc] / invol[a]vit non p[er]mit/tatu . . .nis[i] inn[o]cen/tiam ulla[m] . . ." Reverse: "non illi dimitta[s] / nec somnum nisi ut TATIGIA m[o]dium ne/bulae modium veni/[at] fumi."

Translation: "Whether boy or girl, whether man or woman, the person who has stolen it is not to be permitted . . .unless any innocence . . .you are not to grant him nor sleep unless that . . . a bushel of cloud, an bushel of smoke may come."

Size: 75 x 45mm; Material: Alloy sheet; Holes/Nails: Neither; Location/ Date Found: 1880 in the spring under the King's Bath; Deities: None; Names: None; Reason for Curse: Theft; Other: Written in fourth century script. [534]

65. Peculiar Fragment

Original: "si uapesurusmiimiiii / ille si ceriasius si / igeunsnser per/maneat"

Translation: "Whether . . .let him remain."

Size: 64 x 55mm; Material: Tin alloy sheet; Holes/Nails: Neither; Location/ Date Found: In the spring under the King's Bath; Deities: None; Names: None; Reason for Curse: Unknown; Other: Folded once.[535]

---

[532] Tomlin, "The Curse Tablets," 206, no. 71.

[533] Tomlin, "The Curse Tablets," 213, no. 78.

[534] Tomlin, "The Curse Tablets," 236, no. 100 and Collingwood, *Roman Inscriptions of Britain* I #2349.

[535] Tomlin, "The Curse Tablets," 238, no. 101.

66. The Name of the Thief

Original: "nomen fur/ti si se[rv]us / si l[ibe]r / si puer si pue/lla . . ."

Translation: "The name of the thief, whether slave or free, whether boy or girl. . ."

Size: 38 x 53mm; Material: Tin/lead alloy sheet; Holes/Nails: Neither; Location/ Date Found: In the spring under the King's Bath; Deities: None; Names: None; Reason for Curse: Theft; Other: Folded. [536]

67. Ultimate Penalty

Transpositioned Latin Version: ". . . modsusio . . . iuiuci / deus faci[a]t ani[m]am / pe[r]d[e]re sui"

Translation: ". . . may the god make him lose his life."

Size: 66 x 27mm; Material: Lead/tin alloy; Holes/Nails: Neither; Location/ Date Found: In the spring under the King's Bath; Deities: None; Names: None; Reason for Curse: Vengeance.[537]

68. Theft

Original: ". . . doscim . . . / verit si ser/[vus si liber] . . ." Reverse: ". . . / . . . m fecerit . . ./ . . . intelleg . . ."

Translation: "whether slave or free . . . has done . . . understand . . ."

Size: 53 x 52mm; Material: Tin/lean alloy sheet; Holes/Nails: Neither; Location/ Date Found: In the spring under the King's Bath; Deities: none; Names: None; Reason for Curse: Probably theft; Other: Folded four times. [538]

69. Fragment

Original: ". . . m qui mi[hi] . . ."

Translation: ". . . who I . . ."

Size: 41 x 23mm; Material: Unknown; Holes/Nails: Neither; Location/ Date Found: In spring under the King's Bath; Deities: None; Names: None; Reason for Curse: Unknown.[539]

70. Still Folded

Original: "Docime[edis] . .. / de[ae] su[li] . . ./ . . .n . . ."

Translation: "Docimedis . . . the goddess Sulis . . ."

---

[536] Tomlin, "The Curse Tablets," 239 no. 102.

[537] Tomlin, "The Curse Tablets," 240, no. 103.

[538] Tomlin, "The Curse Tablets," 242, no. 105.

[539] Tomlin, "The Curse Tablets," 244, no. 107.

Size: 27 x 31mm; Material: Unknown; Holes/Nails: Neither; Location/ Date Found: In spring under the King's Bath; Deities: Sulis; Names: Docimedis; Reason for Curse: Unknown; Other: Still folded. [540]

Billingford
71. A Different Kind of Magic
Original: "[kharaktreres] / ιαω / αβρασαχ / πανεη αβλαν/ναθαυαlba / δαθε σαλνθεμ / ετ νικθωριαμ / tib[erium] clau[diu]m similem quem pe/perit heren[n]ia marcellia."
Translation: "Iao, Abrasax . . . alblanathanalba, give health and victory to Tiberius Claudius Similis whom Herennia Marcellina bore."
Size: 41.5 x 30mm; Material: 22 carat gold; Holes/Nails: Neither; Location/ Date Found: 2003 in a garden; Deities: Iao (Greek/Gnostic form of Yahweh); Names: Tiberius Claudius Similis, Herennia Marcellina; Reason for Curse: Health and Victory; Other: Folded six times; not a traditonal "curse tablet" in that it does not seek to harm anyone, but it used methods similar to those in other curse tablets, the use of gold, Greek, and Latin, the Greek/Gnostic works Iao and Abrasax, along with many *kharakteres* suggests the creator of the tablet was of Mediterrian origins, as it was alomst identical to many other tablets found in the Mediterrianean world, but incredibly dissimar to Romano-British tablets.[541]

Brean Down
72. *Caricula*
Original: ". . . / caricula quae [si s]er/[v]u[s i] liber si ba[ro] s[i muli]er / qui . . . [d]omin/a . . . facias / sic [i]llas [re]dim[a]t sa[n]guin[e s]uo lier / . . . si bar[o] mu/ . . . "
Translation: ". . . I give to you the *caricula* which I have lost. Whether slave or free, whether man or woman who . . . Lady . . . you are make redeem them thus with his own blood . . . whether man or woman . . ."
Size: 85 x 57 mm; Material: Sheet of lead; Holes/Nails: Neither; Location/ Date Found: 1980 on the beach by Roman temple; Deities: None; Names: None; Reason for Curse: Theft of a *caricula* (exact meaning unknown, possibly and expenisve comb or a misspelling of *caracella*); Other: Folded twice; written in new cursive, suggesting fourth century dating; virtually illegible.[542]

---

[540] Tomlin, "The Curse Tablets," 245, no. 108.

[541] B. C. Burnham, F. Hunter, A. P. Fitzpatrick, S. Worrell, M. W. C. Hassall, and R. S. O. Tomlin "Roman Britain in 2005," *Britannia* 37 (2006): 481-482.

[542] Frere, et al, "Roman Britain in 1985," 433-435.

Brandon

73. Theft of an Iron Pan

Original: "SERADVASORISDVAS / s[i] ser[v]us si anc[i]l[l]a si libertus si] / liberta, si m[u]lie[r] / si baro, popia[m] fer[re]a[m] / EAENEC furtum fece/r[it] dominio Neptuno cor[u]lo pare[n]ta[tu]r"

Translation: "Whoever . . . whether male slave or female slave, whether freedman or freedwoman, whether woman or man . . . has committed the theft of an iron pan he is sacrificed to the lord Neptune with hazel"

Size: 57 x 40mm; Material: Sheet of lead; Holes/Nails: Neither; Location/ Date Found: 1979 in the Little Ouse river; Deities: Neptune; Names: None; Reason for Curse: Theft of an iron pan; Other: In new cursive, suggesting fourth century dating.[543]

Caerleon

74. Nemesis

Original: "Dom[i]na Ne/mesis do ti/bi palleum / et galliculas / qui tulit non / redimat no / uita Sanguiene / sui"

Translation: "Lady Nemesis, I give thee a cloak and a pair of boots; let him who wore them not redeem them except with the life of his Blood-red charger."

Size: 3 ¼ x 3 inches; Material: Lead plate; Holes/Nails: Two nail holes; Location/ Date Found: 1927 in the Roman amphitheater; Deities: Nemesis; Names: None; Reason for Curse: Either theft of a cloak and boots or sabotaging an opponent.[544]

Caistor St. Edmund

75. Several Stolen Goods

Original: "A Nase . . . / eve[h]it Vroc . . . / sius fascia[m] et armi[lla]/s cap[t]olare / spectr[um] / cufia[m] duas ocrias x vas / a stagnea si mascel si me/mina / si puer / si pu[e]lla duas / ocri[as] si vull[u]eris factae sang[uine] / suo ut [i]llu[m] requeratat Neptu[nu]s / e[t] amictus e[t] cufina [et] arm[i]lla[e] / denarri sv cap[t]olare tunc sanguine[e] / fasciam tenet fur e / carta s[upra] s[scripta] ratio[n]e"

---

[543] B. C. Burnham, L. J. F. Keppie, A. S. Esmonde Bleary, M. W. C. Hassall, and R. S. O. Tomlin "Roman Britain in 1993," *Britannia* 25 (1994): 293-294.

[544] Collingwood, *Roman Inscriptions of Britain* I #323.

Translation: ". . . carries off from Nase . . . a wreath, bracelets, a cap, a mirror, a headdress, a pair of leggings, ten pewter vessels, whether he be man or woman, boy or girl. If you Neptune shall have wished for the pair of leggings, they shall become yours at the price of his blood, so that he, Neptune, shall seek him out, and a cloak and head-dress and bracelets, fifteen denarii, the cap. Then the thief holds onto the wreath at the cost of his blood in accordance with the transaction on the above written sheet."
Size: 105 x 65mm; Material: Lead; Holes/Nails: Neither; Location/ Date Found: 1981 on the bank of the river Tas; Deities: Neptune; Names: Nase; Reason for Curse: Theft of a wreath, bracelets, a cap, a mirror, a headdress, a pair of leggings, and ten pewter vessels. Other: Tablet was tightly rolled up, poorly written.[545]

Chesterton
76. Diogenis
Original: ". . .[D]iogen[i]s dalmatuc[um] / seithaus . . . / dalmaticum"
Translation: ". . . Diogenis . . . "
Size: 2 3/16 x 1 ¼ inches; Material: Lead; Holes/Nails: Neither; Location/ Date Found: 1922 under the Roman fort; Deities: None; Names: Diogenes; Reason for Curse: Unknown; Other: Folded once, includes three lines of capital text and several lines of mostly illegible cursive text superimposed. [546]

Clothall
77. Tacita is Labeled
Transpositioned Latin Version: "uetus / quodmodo sanies / significatur / Tacita deficta"
Translation: "Tacita, hereby accursed, is labeled old like putrid gore."
Size: 4 34/ x 4 inches; Material: Lead; Holes/Nails: Five nail holes and four iron nails; Location/ Date Found: 1930 in a Romano-British cemetery in Walls Field near an urn; Deities: None; Names: Tacita; Reason for Curse: Unknown; Other: Written right to left.[547]

Dodford, Northampton
78. Theft

---

[545] Rankov, et al, "Roman Britain in 1981," 408-409.

[546] Collingwood, *Roman Inscriptions of Britain* I #243 and S. S. Frere, M W. C. Hassall, and R. S. O. Tomlin, "Roman Britain in 1988," *Britannia* 20 (1989): 344-345.

[547] Collingwood, *Roman Inscriptions of Britain* I #221. Translation by Collingwood.

Original: "... mneui ... cl ... ni c[u]m / ... pluminono ... telo ... at / ... su[a] . . . s ... silomo ... / cui ... rliomi ... q / opoulnsllm ... na / pocciapuoiico ... tcs / marinan ... rt / masus ... msaso / si s ... jsnsus / ... ns"

Translation: "... not with / ... reveal ... you ... / ... his own property... if ... / who ... / marine ... / stays .. / if ..."

Size: 89 x 72 mm; Material: Lead sheet; Holes/Nails: None; Location/ Date Found: 2005; Deities: None; Names: None; Reason for Curse: Theft;[548]

Eccles Villa

79. Butu

Reconstructed Latin Version: "donatio diebus quo / perit Butu resque / qu[a]e . . nec ante da/netate nec salute / nesi qua[m] in dopm[o die / ... sanetate in do/[mo de]" Reverse: "s[...] s[upra] s[crip]ti"

Translation: "A gift to the gods by which Butu has perished, and the property which ... neither health nor safety before unless in the house of God ... health in the house of God, in the house of God."

Size: 89 x 71mm; Material: Lead sheet; Holes/Nails: Neither; Location/ Date Found: 1970 under room 212 of the villa; Deities: God; Names: Butu; Reason for Curse: Probably theft; Other: Folded several times, late Roman cursive, suggesting fourth century dating, alternate lines were inverted. [549]

Farley Heath

80. Theft of 4000 *Denarii*

Original Inner Text: "deo DaVIIS . . . Senislis / Senii . . ." Outer Text: "[denariis] III milibus . . [Aur]elius Se . . . / . . .us . . ."

Translated Inner Text: "To the god . . . Senilis son of Sennus" Outer Text: "At four thousand denarii . . . Aurelius Se. . ."

Size: 125 x 17mm; Material: Sheet of lead; Holes/Nails: Neither; Location/ Date Found: 1995 at the Roman temple; Deities: None; Names: Senilis, Sennus, Aurelius; Reason for Curse: Theft of 4000 *denarii*; Other: Tablet remains in a still folded state.[550]

---

[548] E. M. Chapman, F. Hunter, P. Booth, P. Wilson, S., Worrell and R. S. O. Tomlin "Roman Britain in 2008," *Britannia* 40 (2009): 347.

[549] Frere, et al, "Roman Britain in 1985," 428.

[550] B. C. Burnham, F. Hunter, A. P. Fitzpatrick, S. Worrell, M. W. C. Hassall, and R. S. O. Tomlin "Roman Britain in 2003," *Britannia* 35 (2004): 335-336.

Hamble Estuary
81. Silver and Gold
Original: "domine neptune / t[i]b[i] d[o]no [h]ominem qui / [solidum] involav[it] mu/coni et argenti[olo]s / sex ide[o] dono nomi[n]a / qui decepit si mascelt si / femina si puuer si puue/lla ideo dono tibi niske / et neptuno vitam vali/tudinem sanguem eius / qui conscius fueris eius / deceptionis animus / qui hoc involavit et / qui conscius fuerit ut / eum hoc involavit sanguem / eiius consumas et de/cipias domin[e] ne[p]/tune"
Translation: "Lord Nepturne, I give you the man who has stolen the *solidus* and six *argentioli* of Muconius. So I give the names who took them away, whether male or female, whether boy or girl. So I give you, Niskus, and to Neptune the life, health, and blood of him who has been pricy to that taking-away. The mind which stole this and which has been privy to it, may you take it away. The thief who stole this, may you consume his blood and take it away, Lord Neptune."
Size: 84 x 128mm; Material: Sheet of lead; Holes/Nails: Neither; Location/ Date Found: 1982 on the shore; Deities: Neptune, Niskus; Names: Muconius; Reason for Curse: Theft of a *solidus* and six *argentioli*, which were gold and silver pieces; Other: Found rolled up, fourth century cursive. [551]

Hereford and Worcester
82. Possible Curse Tablet
Original: "C. CNOVILL.S."
Size: 140 x 350mm; Material: Pewter plate; Holes/Nails: Neither; Location/ Date Found: in 1980 in the Blackwardine area; Deities: None; Names: None; Reason for Curse: Unknown; Other: Crude picture of a naked woman, suggesting that it might be some sort of love curse. [552]

Kelvedon
83. Mercury and Virtue
Original: "Quicumque res Careni in/volaverit si mulrer si mascel / sangu[i]no suo solvat erit / et pecunie quam exesu/Mercurio dona et Virtuti s[acra]"
Translation: "Whoever has stolen the property of Varenus, whether woman or man, in his own blood and from the money which he has consumed let him pay gifts to Mercury and sacred offerings to Virtue."

---

[551] Frere, et al, "Roman Britain in 1985," 455-457.

[552] Grew, et al, "Roman Britain in 1980,"385-386.

Size: 4 ½ x 1 9/10 inches; Material: Lead; Holes/Nails: Neither; Location/ Date Found: 1956 in an oven; Deities: Mercury, Virtue; Names: Varenus; Reason for Curse: Theft.[553]

Leicester

84. Long List of Suspects

Original: "daeo Maglo [do] euum qui frudum / fecit de padoio [do] elameum qui / furtum [fecit] de padaoium saum / qui sa[g]um Sevandi involva/vit / S[il]vester Ri[g]omandus / S[e]nilis Venustinus / Vorena / Calaminus / Felicianus / Rufaedo / Vendicina / Ingenuinus / Iuventius / Alocus / Cennosus / Germanus / Senedo / Cunovendus / Regalis / Ni[g]ella / S[enic]ianus / [do] antae nonum diem / illum tollat / qui tollat / qui sa[g]um involauit / Servandi."

Translation: "I give to the god Maglus him who did wrong from the slave quarters. I give him who did theft the cloak from the slave quarters, who stole the cloak of Servandus: Silvester, Rigomandus, Senilis, Venustinus, Vorvena, Calaminus, Felicianus, Rufaedo, Vendicina, Ingeniunus, Iuventius, Alocus, Cennosus, Germanus, Sendo, Cunovendus, Regalis, Nigella, Senicianus. I give that the god Maglus before the ninth day take away him who stole the cloak of Servandus."

Size: 78 x 201 mm; Material: Lead Sheet; Holes/Nails: Neither; Location/ Date Found: 2005 in a courtyard of a Roman home; Deities: Maglus; Names: Servandus, Silvester, Rigomandus, Senilis, Venustinus, Vorvena, Calaminus, Felicianus, Rufaedo, Vendicina, Ingeniunus, Iuventius, Alocus, Cennosus, Germanus, Sendo, Cunovendus, Regalis, Nigella, Senicianus; Reason for Curse: Theft of a cloak; Other: The name Senicianus, while still legible, was deleted by the author.[554]

85. Theft of Silver Coins

Original: "qu[ia]rgentios Sabiniani fura/verunt id est Similis Cupitus Lochita / hos deus siderabit in hoc septiso/nio et peto ut vitam suam per/dant ante dies septem"

Translation: "Those who have stolen the silver coins of Sabiniaus, that is Similis, Cupitus, Lochita, a god will strike down in this septisonum, and I ask that they lose thier life before seven days."

---

[553] Society for the Promotion of Roman Studies. "Roman Britain in 1957: I. Sites Explored: II. Inscriptions," *The Journal of Roman Studies* 48, no.1/2 (1958): 150.

[554] Chapman, et al, "Roman Britain in 2008," 327-328.

Size: 123 x 69 mm; Material: Lead Sheet; Holes/Nails: Neither; Location/ Date Found: Unknown; Deities: Not specifically given; Names: Sabiniaus, Similis, Cupitus, Lochita; Reason for Curse: Stolen Silver Coins.[555]

Leintwardine

86. Seven Names
Original: "Carinus / Similis / Consortius / Comes Masloriu[s] / Senorix Cunittus / Cunittus Cunedecan / ES / Ceanatis Tiberin[us]"
Size: 3 4/5 x 2 ¼ inches; Material: Lead; Holes/Nails: Neither; Location/ Date Found: 1964 in the bathhouse of a Roman fort; Deities: None; Names: Carinus, Similis, Consortius, Comes Maslorius, Senorix Cunittus, Cunittus Cunedecan, Ceanatis Tiberinus; Reason for Curse: Unknown.[556]

87. Three Names
Original: "Enestinus / Motius / Comintinus."
Size: 2 3/5 x 11/12 inches; Material: Lead; Holes/Nails: Neither; Location/ Date Found: 1964 in the bathhouse of a Roman fort; Deities: None; Names: Enestinus, Motius, Comintinus; Reason for Curse: Unknown.[557]

London

88. Tretia Maria
Original: "Tretia[m] Maria[m] defico et / illeus uita[m] et me[n]tem / et memoriam [e]t iocine / ra pulmones interm xixi / ta fata cogitata meor/iam sci no[no] possitt loqui / [quae] sicreta si[n]t neque SINTA / MERE posit neque . . / . . . CL V DO"
Translation: "I curse Tretia Maria and her life and mind and memory and liver and lungs mixed up together, and her words, thoughts and memory; thus may she be unable to speak what things are concealed, nor be able . . ."
Size: 7 x 4 ¾ inches; Material: Lead sheet; Holes/Nails: Several nail holes; Location/ Date Found: 1934 on Telegraph St., Moorgate; Deities: None; Names: Tretia Maria; Reason for Curse: Unknown. [558]

---

[555] Chapman, et al, "Roman Britain in 2008," 329.

[556] D. R.Wilson and R. P. Wright, "Roman Britain in 1968: I. Sites Explored: II. Inscriptions," *The Journal of Roman Studies* 59 no.1/2 (1969): 241.

[557] Wilson and Wright, "Roman Britain in 1968," 241.

[558] Collingwood, *Roman Inscriptions of Britain* I #7.

89. The 'London Curse'
Original: "T[itus] Egnatius / Tyran[n]us defic[t]tus / est et / P[ublius] Cicereius Felix / defictus e[st]" Reverse: "T[itus] Egnatius / Tyran[nus] defictus / est et / P[ublius] Cicereius Felix"
Translation: "Titus Egnatius is cursed and Publius Cicereius Felix is cursed."
Size: 4 ¾ x 3 inches; Material: Hammered lead; Holes/Nails: One nail hole; Location/ Date Found: 1928 on Princess Street; Deities: None; Names: Titus Egnatius and Publius Cicereius Felix; Reason for Curse: Unknown.[559]

90. Three Latin Names
Original: "a[u]rel[ius] satir/ninus domitia atti/ola et si qui afuere"
Translation: "Plautius Nobilianus, Aurelius Saturninus, Domitia Attiola, and any who were absent."
Size: 70 x 50mm; Material: Sheet of lead; Holes/Nails: Neither; Location/ Date Found: 1994; Deities: None; Names: Plautius Nobilianus, Aurelius Saturninus, Comitia Attiola; Reason for Curse: Unknown; Other: Folded twice.[560]

91. The Goddess Deana
Original: "[d]eae dea[na]e dono / capitularem et fas/[c]iam minus parte / tertia si quis hoc feci[t] / [s]i p[u]er si [p]uella s[i] / [s]er[vus] s[i liber] / don[o eum] nec p[er] / me [vi]v[ere] possit."
Translation: "I give to the goddess Deana my headgear and band less one-third. If anyone has done this, I give him, and through me let him be unable to live."
Size: 85 x 105mm; Material: Sheet of lead; Holes/Nails: Neither; Location/ Date Found: 1992 in the drain of the Roman amphitheatre; Deities: Deana; Names: None; Reason for Curse: Theft of headgear.[561]

92. London Bridge Tablet
Original: "tibi rogo Metu/nus u[t] m[e] vendic/as de iste nu/mene me ven/dicas ante q[u]o/d ven[iant] die[s] no/vem rogo te / Metunus ut [t]u / mi vend[i]cas / ante q[u]o[d] / ven[iant] di[es] n[o]ve/m." Reverse: "xuparanti / silvielesatavile / xsuparatus Silvico/le Avitus Melus/so datus / perucitibi / Santinus / Magetus / apidimis Antoni / Santus Varia/nus Varasius datus"

---

[559] Collingwood, *Roman Inscriptions of Britain* I #6.

[560] B. C. Burnham, F. Hunter, A. P. Fitzpatrick, M. W. C. Hassall, and R. S. O. Tomlin, "Roman Britain in 2002," *Britannia* 34 (2003): 361.

[561] Burnham, et al, "Roman Britain in 2002," 362.

Translation: "I ask you Metunus/Neptune, that you avenge me on this name that you avenge me before nine days come. I ask you, Metunus/Neptune, that you avenge me before nine days come."
Size: 69 x 95mm; Material: Sheet of lead; Holes/Nails: Neither; Location/ Date Found: 1984 on the north shore of the Themes; Deities: Neptune; Names: Silvico, Avitus, Melusso, Santinus, Magetus, Antoni, Santus, Varianus, Varasius, and several possible names; Reason for Curse: Revenge for unspecified event; Other: Reverse side is chaotic and the "S"s on both sides were written backwards.[562]

Lydney Park
93. Silvianus's Ring
Original: "Devo / Nodenti Siluianus / anilum perdedit / demediam partme / donauit Nodenti / inter quibus nomen / Seniciani nollis / petmittas anita / tem donec perfera / usque templum / [No]dentis" Secondary text: "Rediuiua"
Translation: "To the god Nodens. Silvianus has lost his ring and given half to Noden. Among those who are called Senicianus do not allow health until it is brought to the temple of Nodens."
Size: 2 ½ x 2 1/8 inches; Material: Bronze; Holes/Nails: Neither; Location/ Date Found: 1817 in the temple of Nodens; Deities: Nodens; Names: Silvianus; Reason for Curse: Theft of a gold ring;[563] Other: Ironically a gold ring was found in Silchester with the following found inscribed on it: "Seniciaunus, live in God."[564]

Marlborough Downs
94. Invocation to Mars
Original: " do a / deo Marti A . . . VNISEA id [est] . . ./ eculium eum et secur. . . / tidissee . . . illum iume . . . / rogat genium tuum domine / ut quampri[imu]m res[ideant] / nec eant per annos novem n[on eis] / permittas nec sedere [nec. . .] / . . ..MIMBRIC . . ."
Translation: "I give . . . to you god Mars . . . asks your Genius, Lord, that they stop as soon as possible and do not go for nine years. Do not allow them to sit or . . ."
Size: 72 x 49mm; Material: Sheet of lead; Holes/Nails: Neither; Location/ Date Found: 1998 in the topsoil; Deities: Mars; Names: None; Reason for Curse: Unknown; Other: folded. [565]

---

[562] Frere, et al, "Roman Britain in 1986," 360-362.

[563] Collingwood, *Roman Inscriptions of Britain* I #306.

[564] Collingwood, *Roman Inscriptions of Britain* II #2422.14.

[565] Keppie, et al, "Roman Britain in 1998," 378-379.

Malton

95. Possible Curse Tablet

Original: "ISARSES / COVIS / AEEO / CECEX" Reverse: "ISVXOSIS"

Size: 35 x 27mm; Material: Lead sheet; Holes/Nails: Neither; Location/ Date Found: 1969 south of the Malton fort; Deities: None; Names: None; Reason for Curse: Unknown.[566]

Old Harlow

96. Eterna and Timotneus

Original: "Dio M[ercurio] dono ti[bi] / negotium Et/[t]ern[a]e et ipsam / nec sit i[n]vidi[a] me[i] / Timotneo san/gui[n]e suo." Reverse: "Dono tibi / Mercurius / aliam neg[o]/tium NAVIN / . . . / NII . . . / MIN . . . SANG / SVO"

Translation: "To the god Mercury, I entrust to you my affair with Eterna and her own self and may Timotneus feel no jealousy of me at the risk of his life-blood." Reverse: "I entrust to you, O Mercury, another transaction . . ."

Size: 54 x 72mm; Material: Lead sheet; Holes/Nails: Holes and nail found; Location/ Date Found: 1970 in pit or well at Holbrooks; Deities: Mercury; Names: Eterna and Timotneus; Reason for Curse: Love affair or business transaction; Other: neat capital letters, found with third/fourth century pottery.[567]

Oxford

97. Protection for a Child

Original: "(three lines of charakteres) ϛαμιου / Ηριϛφαλμα χνουν / ιαχματιαν φνε / φνε ωχ ποιηϲα / τε τοῖς (ὑ)μετέροις / ἁγίοις ὀνόμαϲι / ἵνα τὸ ἔ(γ)κυον / κρατής(ει) καὶ τεξετ(αι) / ὁλοκληρούϲα καὶ / ὑγι(αί)νουϲα Φάβι/α ἥν ἔτεκεν Τερέ(ν)/τια μήτηρ (αἰεὶ) ὀνό/ματος τοῦ κυρίου / καὶ μεγάλου θεοῦ"

Translation: "Make with your holy names that Fabis, whom Terentia her mother bore, being in full fitness and health, shall master the unborn child and bring it to birth, the name of the Lord and Great God being everlasting."

---

[566] D. R. Wilson, R. P. Wright, and M. W. C. Hassall, "Roman Britain in 1970," *Britannia* 2 (1971): 302-303.

[567] D. R. Wilson, R. P. Wright, and M. W. C. Hassall, "Roman Britain in 1972," *Britannia* 4 (1973): 325-327. Translation by R. P. Wright and M. W. C. Hassall.

Size: 28 x 63 mm; Material: Impure gold leaf; Holes/Nails: Neither; Location/ Date Found: 2007 in the ploughsoil; Deities: God ; Names: Fabia, Terentia; Reason for Curse: Protection for mother and child ; Other: Like the Billingford tablet, this gold luck charm is radically different from the other Romano-British tablets, suggesting a non-native author; the tablet includes several *charakteres* and is the only tablet to utalize only Greek.[568]

Pagan's Hill
98. Theft of Three Thousand *Denarii*
Original: " . . . mitr . . . pio . . . / in is iii milibus cuius [de]mediam / partem tibi ut ita illum [e]xigas a Vassicil/lo . . pecomini filio et uxore sua quoniam . . . . rtussum quod illi de hopitiolo m[eo] / . . .ulaverint nec illis [p]ermittas sanit[a]/[tem] nec bibere nec man[n]d[u]care nec dormi[re] / [nec nat]os sanos habe[a]nt nessi hanc rem / [meam] ad fanum tuum [at]tulerint iteratis / [pre]c[i]bus te rogo ut [ab ip]sis nominibus / [inimicorum] meorum hoc [pertu]ssum recipi / . . . perven[ia]t"

Translation: ". . . in three thousand *denarii*, of which I give you half part on condition that you exact it from Vassicillus the son of . . .cominus and from his wife, since the coin which they have stolen from my house . . . and you are not to permit them health nor to drink nor to eat nor to sleep nor to have healthy children unless they bring this property to your temple. With repeated prayers I ask you that this may come to be recovered from the names of my enemies."

Size: 95 x 101mm; Material: Sheet of lead; Holes/Nails: Neither; Location/ Date Found: 1983; Deities: None; Names: Vassicillus; Reason for Curse: The theft of three thousand *denarii*.[569]

99. Eight Times Nine
Original: ". . . gno . . quem / . . . tuadrodit . . . / . . .t . . ./ . . .q. . ./ octies novem e / sit omni gen / borum fatigatu / e exorit . . s . . ."

Translation: ". . . eight times nine . . . let him be wearied with every sort of hardships."

Size: 75 x 45mm; Material: Sheet of lead; Holes/Nails: Neither; Location/ Date Found: 1983; Deities: None; Names: None; Reason for Curse: Unknown.[570]

---

[568] Chapman, et al, "Roman Britain in 2008," 353-354. Translation by Tomlin.

[569] Burnham, et al, "Roman Britain in 1983," 336 and 339 and S. S. Frere, S. S. and R. S. O. Tomlin, "Roman Britain in 1990," *Britannia* 22 (1991): 309.

[570] Frere, et al, "Roman Britain in 1983," 336 and 340.

100. Fragment
Original: ". . . cond . . . tin . . . / . . . umqu[e] quomin[us . . .] / . . . fra[d]e sua ul[la . . .] / . . . us donav . . . / . . . eus . . ."
Translation: ". . . and less . . . any of his . . ."
Size: 15 x 52mm; Material: Sheet of lead; Holes/Nails: Neither; Location/ Date Found: 1983; Deities: None; Names: None; Reason for Curse: Unknown.[571]

Puckeridge-Braughing
101. Symbol
Size: 147 x 55mm; Material: Sheet of lead; Holes/Nails: Pierced with nails five times; Location/ Date Found: 1972; Deities: None; Names: None; Reason for Curse: Unknown; Other: folded several times, one side has only a symbol, the other side is illegible.[572]

Ratcliffe-on-Soar
102. Prayer to Jupiter
Original: "donatur deo Ioui / optimo maximo ut / exigat per mentem per / memoriam per intus / per intestinum per cor / [p]er medullas per uenas / per . . . as / . . . . si mascel si / femina quisquis." Reverse: "inuolauit rios Cani / Digni ut in corpore / suo in breui temp[or]e / pariat donatur / deo ssto decima pars / eius pecuniae quam / [so]luerit."
Translation: "To Jupiter, Greatest and Best, there is given that he hound through his mind, through his memory, through his innards, through his intestines, through his heart, through his marrow, through his veins, through . . . whoever it was, whether man or woman who stole the denarii of Canius Dignus, that in his own person he may shortly settle his debt. The god is granted a tenth of the money, when it is repaid it."
Size: 8.4 x 5.7cm; Material: Lead; Holes/Nails: Neither; Location/ Date Found: 1960 on Red Hill; Deities: Jupiter; Names: Canius Dignus; Reason for Curse: Theft of money; Other: Folded thrice. [573]

103. Theft of a Mule or Millstone
Originally: "nomine Camulorigi[s] et Titocun[a]e molam quam perdederunt / in fanum dei devovi cuicumque n[o]m[e]n involasit / mola[m] illam ut

---

[571] Frere, et al, "Roman Britain in 1983," 336 and 341.

[572] Frere, et al, "Roman Britain in 1985," 436-437.

[573] Eric G. Turner, "A Curse from Nottinghamshire," *The Journal of Roman Studies* 53, no. 1/2 (1963): 122-123.

sa[n]guin[em] suum mittat usque diem quo / moriatur q[ui]cumque invo[l]a[sit] [f]urta moriatur / et PAVLAVTORIAM quicumque illam involasit / et ipse moriato mo[ri]atur quicumqu[e] illam / involasit et VERTIGN de [h]ospitio vel vissacio . quicumque illam involasit a devo mori[a]tur."

Translation: "In the name of Camulorix and Titocuna I have dedicated in the temple of the god the mule/millstone(?) they lost. Whoever stole that mule/millstone, whatever his name, let him pour out his blood to the day he dies. Whoever stole the items of theft, may he die, and whoever stole the . . . may he die too. Whoever stole it and the . . . from the house or the pair of bags, whoever stole it, may he die by the god."

Size: 112 x 56mm; Material: Sheet of lead; Holes/Nails: Neither; Location/ Date Found: 1990 in a field; Deities: None; Names: Camulorix and Titocuna; Reason for Curse: Theft of either a mule or millstone; Other: Letters were written in mirror image from right to left.[574]

104. Theft of Several Items

Original: "annoto de duas / ocrias ascia[m] scal/pru[m] ma[n]ica[m] si m[ulier] au[t] si / b[aro] RIANTINE duas / partis deo AC CEVM."

Translation: "I make a not of two gaiters, and axe, a knife, a pair of gloves, whether woman or if man . . . two parts to the god."

Size: 82 x 38mm; Material: Lead; Holes/Nails: Neither; Location/ Date Found: 1963 at the site of a Roman temple; Deities: None; Names: None; Reason for Curse: Theft of gaiters, an ace, a knife, and a pair of gloves. Other: handwriting suggests fourth century.[575]

Silchester

105. Suspects in Theft

Transpositioned Original: "Nimincillus [Quintinus] / lu[n]ctinus D[o]cillinae / lon[g]intus VSCANIMIHMS / . . . NIS. . . IC. . . eu[m] / qui invalaveri/t deus det ma/la[m] plagam."

Translation: "Nimincillus, Quintinus, Iunctinus son of Docillina, Longinus . . . Him who has stolen, let the gid give a nasty blow."

[574] B. C. Burnham, L. J. F. Keppie, A. S. Esmonde Bleary, M. W. C. Hassall, and R. S. O. Tomlin. "Roman Britain in 1992," *Britannia* 24 (1993): 310-312.

[575] Burnham, et al, "Roman Britain in 2003," 336-337.

Size: 60 x 103mm; Material: Lead sheet; Holes/Nails: two holes; Location/ Date Found: Before 1901; Deities: None; Names: Nimincillus, Quintinus, Iunctinus, Docillina, Longinus; Reason for Curse: Theft. Other: Folded twice; Written in reverse; handwriting suggests fourth century.[576]

Thetford
106. Possible Curse Tablet
Original: "OVA / SVINIMEP / SILAVON / MEPTSESV"
Possible interpretation: "[defix]us est Pem[inius]"
Size: 53 x 46mm; Material: Irregular sheet of lead; Holes/Nails: Neither; Location/ Date Found: With the Thetford treasure hoard; Deities: None; Names: None; Reason for Curse: Unknown.[577]

Uley
107. Lost Linen
Original: "Commonitorium deo / Mercurio a Satur/nina muliere de lintia/mine quod amisit ut il/le qui hoc circumvenit non / ante laxetur nisi quando / res ssdictas ad fanum ssdic/tum attulerit si vir si mu/lier si servus s[i] liber."
Reverse: "Deo ssdicto tertiam / partem donat ita ut / ex sigat istas re quae / ssta[e] sunt / Ac a quae perit deo Silvano / tertia pars donatur ita ut /hoc exsigat si vir si femina si ser/us si liber . . . E . . . TAT."
Translation: "A memorandum to the god Mercury from Saturnina a woman concerning the linen cloth she has lost. Let him who stole it not have rest before/unless/until he brings the aforesaid things to the aforesaid temple, whether he is a man or a woman, slave or free." Reverse: "She gives a third part to the aforesaid god on condition that he exact those things which have been aforewritten. A third part from what has been lost is given to the god Silvanus on condition that he exact this, whether the thief is man or woman, slave or free."
Size: 83 x 60mm; Material: Lead; Holes/Nails: Neither; Location/ Date Found: 1977 at the temple on West Hill; Deities: Mercury and Mars-Silvanus; Names: Saturnia; Reason for Curse: Theft of linen; Other: Folded four times, Mars-Silvanus is scratched out and replaced by Mercury.[578]

---

[576] Chapman, et al, "Roman Britain in 2008," 323-324.

[577] Rankov, et al, "Roman Britain in 1981," 410.

[578] R. Goodburn, M W. C. Hassall, R. S. O. Tomlin, "Roman Britain in 1978," *Britannia* 10 (1979): 343- 344.

108. Stolen Animal
Original: "Deo Mercurio / Cenacus queritur / de Vitalino et Nat/lino filio ipsius d[e] / iumento quod erap/tum est. Erogat / deum Mercurium / ut nec ante sa/nitatem." Reverse: "habeant nisi / nisi repraese[n]/taverint mihi iu/mentum quod r[a]/puerunt et deo devotionem qua[m] / ipse ab his ex/postulaverit." Translation: "Canacus complains to the god Mercury about Vitalinus and Natalinus his son concerning the stolen draught animal. He begs the god Mercury that they may neither have health . . . unless they repay me promptly for the animal they have stolen and the god the devotion which he himself has demanded of them."
Size: 85 x 135mm; Material: Lead; Holes/Nails: Neither; Location/ Date Found: 1977 at the temple on West Hill; Deities: Mercury; Names: Vitalinus and Natalinus; Reason for Curse: Stolen draft animal. [579]

109. Biccus's Vengeance
Original: "Biccus dat M/ercuri quidquid / pe[r]d[di]it si vir si m/ascel ne meiat / ne cavet ne loqu/tur ne dormiat / n[e] vigilet nec s[a]/[l]uetm nec sa/nitatem ne/ss[i] in templo / Mercurri per/tulerit ne co[n]/scientiam de / perferat ness[i] / me intercen/te."
Translation: "Biccus gives to Mercury whatever he has lost on the condition that the thief, whether man or male may not urinate or defecate or speak or sleep or wake or have well-being or health unless he brings it to the temple of Mercury, nor gain consciousness of it unless at my intercession."
Size: 66 x 124mm; Material: Sheet of lead; Holes/Nails: Possibly two nail holes at the bottom; Location/ Date Found: 1978 at the temple of Mercury on West Hill; Deities: Mercury; Names: Biccus; Reason for Curse: Theft; Other: folded several times.[580]

110. Harmed Animal
Original: "deo Mercurio / Docilinus QVAENM / Varianus et Peregrina / et Sabinianus qu[i] perco/ri meo dolum malum in/tulerunt et INT.RR pro/locuntur rogo te ut eos / max[i]mo [le]to adigas nec / eis sanit[atem nec] som/num perm[itt]as nisi / a te quod m[ihi] ad[mi]/ni[strav]erint / rede[e]rint"

---

[579] Goodburn, et al, "Roman Britain in 1978," 340-342.

[580] S. S. Frere, M W. C. Hassall, and R. S. O. Tomlin "Roman Britain in 1987," *Britannia* 19 (1988): 465-487.

Translation: "To the god Mercury. Docilinus . . . Varianus and Peregrina and Sabiniaus who have brought evil harm to my beast and . . . I ask you to drive them to the greatest death and grant them neither health nor sleep unless they redeem from you what they have done to me."
Size: 84x98mm; Material: Hammered lead sheet; Holes/Nails: Neither; Location/ Date Found: 1978 at the temple of Mercury on West Hill; Deities: Mercury; Names: Doilinus, Varianus, Peregrina, Sabinianus; Reason for Curse: Harm of an animal.[581]

111. Stolen Bridle
Original: "nomen furis / [qu]i frenem involaverit / si l[i]ber si sevus si baro / si mulier deo dona/tor duas partes / AFIMA sua ter/tia ad sanita/tem"
Translation: "The name of the thief who has stolen my bridle, whether free or slave, whether man or woman, is given to the god . . . two parts from his wife and a third to his health."
Size: 70 x72mm; Material: Lead sheet; Holes/Nails: Neither; Location/ Date Found: 1978 at the temple of Mercury on West Hill; Deities: None; Names: None; Reason for Curse: Theft of a bridal; Other: Old Roman Cursive is used.[582]

112. Fragment
Original: ". . . / [r]ogo laqu . . ." Reverse: ". . . as date . . . / summam div . . ."
Translation: ". . . I ask . . . give me . . ."
Size: 31 x 18mm; Material: Lead; Holes/Nails: Neither; Location/ Date Found: 1972 masonry building at West Hill; Deities: None; Names: None; Reason for Curse: Theft; Other: Folded several times[583]

113. Theft of a Golden Ring
Original: "Deo M[a]rti Mercur[io] / anulus areus de hos[pitiolo . . . involav]/erit et pedica ferre[a . . .] / s. qui fraudem fec/[it . . / r . . . deus invenit[a]t"
Translation: "To the god Mars-Mercury. . . gold ring from . . . house . . . and iron fetter . . . who did wrong . . . let the god discover.."[584]

---

[581] Frere, et al, "Roman Britain in 1988," 329-330.

[582] Frere, et al, "Roman Britain in 1988," 327-328.

[583] Wilson, et al, "Roman Britain in 1972," 324.

[584] Frere and Tomlin"Roman Britain in 1990," 307-308.

Size: 98 x 54mm; Material: Lead; Holes/Nails: One possible hole; Location/ Date Found: 1977 at the temple on West Hill; Deities: Mars-Mercury; Names: None; Reason for Curse: Theft of a gold ring and iron fetter; Other: Folded twice, has been corrected since first publication.[585]

114. Petronius

Original: "PETRONIIUS"
Size: 85 x 105 mm; Material: Sheet of lead; Holes/Nails: One nail hole; Location/ Date Found: 1978 at the temple of Mercury on West Hill; Deities: None; Names: Petronius; Reason for Curse: Unknown. [586]

115. Stolen Cloak

Original: "deo Mercurio Mintl/a Rufus donavi / eos vel mulier cel / PARIVSLIIFASPATEM / [ma]teriam sagi / donavi"
Translation: "Mintla Rufus to the god Mercury. I have given them, whether woman or man . . . the material of a cloak. I have given them."
Size: 60 x 95 mm; Material: Sheet of lead; Holes/Nails: Neither; Location/ Date Found: 1978 at the temple on West Hill; Deities: Mercury; Names: Mintla Rufus; Reason for Curse: Theft.[587]

116. A Curse Against Enemies

Original: "[deo] sancto Mercuri[o] [que]r[or] / tibi de illis qui mihi male / cogitant et male faciunt / supra EDS iumen / si servus si liber si m[ascel] / si [fem]ina ut non illis per/mittas nec sta[r]e nec / sedere nec bibere." Reverse: "nec manducar[e] n[e]c h[as] / [i]r[a]s redemere possit / nessi sanguine suo AENE"
Translation: "To the holy god Mercury. I complain to you about those who are badly disposed towards me and who are acting badly over . . . whether slave or free, whether male or female. Do not allow them to stand or sit, to drink or eat, or to buy off these provocations unless with their own blood . . ."
Size: 79 x 75 mm; Material: Sheet of lead; Holes/Nails: Neither; Location/ Date Found: 1978 at the temple on West Hill; Deities: Mercury; Names: None; Reason for Curse: Unspecified aggression; Other: Folded twice. [588]

---

[585] Goodburn, et al, "Roman Britain in 1978," 344-345.

[586] Burnham, et al, "Roman Britain in 1992," 310-311.

[587] B. C. Burnham, L. J. F. Keppie, A. S. Esmonde Bleary, M. W. C. Hassall, and R. S. O. Tomlin "Roman Britain in 1994," *Britannia* 26 (1995): 371-373.

[588] Burnham, et al, "Roman Britain in 1994," 373-376.

117. Several Names
Original: "Aunillus / V[ica]riana / Covitius / Mini [filius] dona[t] / Varicillum / Minura / Atavacum"
Translation: "Aunillus, Vicariana, Covitius son of Minus gives Varicillus, Minura, Atavacus"
Size: 42 x 66mm; Material: Sheet of lead; Holes/Nails: Neither; Location/ Date Found: 1978 at the temple on West Hill; Deities: None; Names: Aunillus, Vicariana, Covitius, Minus, Varicillus, Minura, Atavacus; Reason for Curse: Unknown; Other: Folded twice.[589]

118. Lucilia, Daughter of Mellossus
Original: "Lucilia / Mellossi [filia] / AEXSIEVMO / Minu[v]assus / Senebel[l]/enae [filius]"
Translation: "Lucilia daughter of Mellossus . . . Minuvassus son of Senebellena"
Size: 70 x 76mm; Material: Sheet of lead; Holes/Nails: Neither; Location/ Date Found: 1978 at the temple on West Hill; Deities: None; Names: Lucilia, Mellossus, Minuvassus, Senebellena; Reason for Curse: Unknown; Other: Folded twice. [590]

119. Stolen Gloves
Original: "carta qu[a]e merurio dona/tur ut manecilis qui per[i]erunt / ultionem requirat qui illos / invalaviit ut illi sangu[in]em [e]t sanita/tem tolla[t] qui ipsos manicili[o]s tulit / [u]t quantocicius illi pareat quod / deum mercurium r[o]gmus . . ura" Reverse:
q . . os nc u . . . lat"
Translation: "The sheet of lead which is given to Mercury, that he exact vengeance for the gloves which have been lost, that he take blood and health from the person who has stolen them, that he provide what we ask the god Mercury . . . as quickly as possible for the person who has taken these gloves."
Size: 72 x 42mm; Material: Sheet of lead; Holes/Nails: Neither; Location/ Date Found: 1978 at the temple on West Hill; Deities: Mercury; Names: None; Reason for Curse: Theft of gloves; Other: Folded five times.[591]

---

[589] Burnham, et al, "Roman Britain in 1994," 376-377.

[590] Burnham, et al, "Roman Britain in 1994," 378-379.

[591] B. C. Burnham, L. J. F. Keppie, A. S. Esmonde Bleary, M. W. C. Hassall, and R. S. O. Tomlin "Roman Britain in 1995," *Britannia* 27 (1996): 439-440.

120. Rings and a Plate
Original: "IORID . . SONAE. . . /. . . LTELL . . ./. . .ESVNT sup[pe]cti sunt inter. . ./ . .ILLVSI . . . EVSRE . . VMINVENETET . . / lami[l]la una et anulli quator . . ."
Translation: ". . . one piece of silver plate and four rings . . ."
Size: 91x 39mm; Material: Sheet of lead; Holes/Nails: Neither; Location/ Date Found: 1978 at the Temple on West Hill; Deities: None; Names: None; Reason for Curse: Theft of one piece of silver plate and four rings; Other: Tablet had been folded, mostly undecipherable.[592]

Wanborough
121. Vengeance
Original: "epre . . .r . .epeto . . . ./ peto iudicio tuo quo. .d . . . .eculans . . . / tum ne lili permittas bibere nec / [do]rmire nec ambulare neque allam . . . /s gentisue ude ille nascit . . / eita ulla nec alumen . . . / . . . pre . . .uemente loquantur et r . . ./ . . . ugabantur certum sciu . . .t . . ./ si / . . . meuerecameue / . . . meor"
Translation: "I beg . . . that you do not permit him to drink nor eat nor sleep nor walk and that you do not allow any part to remain of him or of the family from which he springs."
Size: 55 x 55mm; Material: Lead sheet; Holes/Nails: Neither; Location/ Date Found: Specifics unknown; Deities: None; Names: None; Reason for Curse: Vengeance.[593]

Weeting-with-Broomhill
122. Theft in Reverse
Original: "s[i] servus si [l]ib[er qu]/i [f]uravit su[st]uli/t [ne ei] dimitte / [male]fic[i]um d[u]m / tu vindi[c]a[s]" Reverse: "ante dies / nov[em] si pa/[g]a[n]is si / mil[e]s [qui] / su[s]tu[l]it"
Translation: "Whoever has stolen it, taken it, whether slave or free, do not forgive him his evil doing until you punish him within nine days, whether civilian or soldier, whoever has taken it."
Size: 60 x 55mm; Material: Sheet of lead; Holes/Nails: Neither; Location/ Date Found: Early 1970s at Hockwold-cum-Wilton; Deities: None; Names: None; Reason for Curse: Theft; Other: Written in mirror image capital letters.[594]

---

[592] L. J. F Keppie, A. S. Esmonde Cleary, M. W. C. Hassall, R. S. O. Tomlin, and Barry C. Burnham "Roman Britain in 1997," *Britannia* 29 (1998): 433-434.

[593] M. W. C. Hassall, D. R. Wilson, R. P. Wright, and J. Rea "Roman Britain in 1971," *Britannia* 3 (1972): 363-365.

[594] Burnham, et al, "Roman Britain in 1993," 296-297.

West Deeping

123. Greek Names

Original: "ma[t]r[i]x [t]i[bi] / dico sede in / tuo loco VO . . / . . S dedit tibi ad/iuro te per Iaω / et per Sabaω et / per Adωnai ne / latus teneas se/d sede in tuo lo/co nec nocea[s] Cleuomedem / [fi]iliam A . . ."

Translation: "Womb, I say to you, stay in your place . . . has given to you. I adjure you by Iaô, and by Savaô and by Adônai, not to hold onto the side, but stay in your place, and not to hurt Cleuomedes daughter of A. . . ."

Size: 54 x 103mm; Material: Sheet of lead; Holes/Nails: Neither; Location/ Date Found: 1994 at the site of a Roman villa; Deities: "Womb," suggesting a mother goddess; Names: Iaô, Savaô, Adônai, Cleuomedes; Reason for Curse: Unclear; Other: New cursive, suggesting fourth century dating, tablet was rolled up. [595]

Unknown location

124. Addressed to Majesty

Original: ". . . amisi oro tuam m[aie] / statem ut firem istum / si ancil [l]a si [p]uer si [puella] / ext[i]ngus . . . ut illi s . . . / cias perduci [r]em ra[ptam] / . . . um et . . ."

Translation: ". . . I have lost . . . I beg your Majesty that you destroy this thief, whether slave woman or boy or girl . . . that you force him to produce the stolen property. . ."

Size: 69 x53mm Material: Sheet of lead; Holes/Nails: Neither; Location/ Date Found: 1983 in Southern Britain, exact location unknown; Deities: None; Names: None; Reason for Curse: Theft; Other: Folded into quarters, in Old Roman Cursive.[596]

125. Stolen Axe

Original: "[do]atur deo Merc[urio si] / q[i]llis involaverit c. . . lam / . . . licinnum nec non alia minutalia / Rocitami si baro si mulier si puel[l]a / si puer si ingenuus si servus n[o]n an[t]e / eum laset quam mimbra [ra]pi manu di/em mortis concutiat e[u]m quui[i] se/curam . . . nnoris involavit EA . . . / AEAPR nec non et ququi res [p]ictor[ia]a[s] / involaverit."

[595] Burnham, et al, "Roman Britain in 1995," 443-445.

[596] Frere, et al, "Roman Britain in 1987," 488-489.

Translation: "Given to the god Mercury, whoever has stolen . . . and other sundries . . . whether man or woman, whether girl or boy, whether free-born or slave. May the god not allow him rest before . . . limbs . . . by hand. . . . day of death . . .may the god torment him who has stolen the axe of . . . and who has stolen the writing things."
Size: 137 x 104mm; Material: Hammered lead sheet; Holes/Nails: Four nail holes; Location/ Date Found: Before 1985, probably in Gloucester or Avon; Deities: Mercury; Names: None; Reason for Curse: Theft of an axe and writing implements.[597]

From outside Britain

Original: "Dea Ataecina Turi/brig Proserpina / per tuam maiestatem / te rogo obsecro / uti vindices quot mihi / furti factum est quisquis / mihi imudavit involavit / minusue fecit eas [res] quiss / tunicas VI . . . [pa]enula / lintea II in[dus]ium cu/ius i c v . . . m ignoro / ia . . . ius / vi"
Translation: "Persephone, by your Majesty I ask, beg and beseech you that you avenge the theft that has been done on me. Whoever has dishonored me, robbed me, diminished me of the property written below: six tunics, two linen wraps . . "
Size: Unknown; Material: marble; Holes/Nails: Neither; Location/ Date Found: Lusitania; Deities: Persephone; Names: None; Reason for Curse: Theft of clothing. [598]

Translation: "I dedicate to the mother of the gods all of the gold pieces which I have lost so that she will seek them out and bring all of them into the clear and those ho have them will be punished in a manner befitting her power, so that she will not be made fun of."
Size: 8.1 x 5.5 cm; Material: Bronze; Holes/Nails: One hole; Location/ Date Found: Probably Phrygia; Deities: Cybele; Names: None; Reason for Curse: Theft of money. [599]

---

[597] Frere and Tomlin, "Roman Britain in 1990," 293-295.

[598] Augustus Audollent, *Defixionum Tabellae*, trans. Marie Henri (Frankfurt: Minerva, 1967) ,122.

[599] Gager, *Curse Tablets and Binding Spells of the Ancient World*, 190-191. Originally in Greek, translated by Gager.

Translation: "Lord Gods Sukonaioi K . . . Lady Goddess Syria Sukona . . . punish, show your power and direct your anger at whoever took and stole the necklace at those who had any knowledge of it, at those who took part in it, whether man or woman." Reverse: "Lord Gods Suonaioi . . . Lady Goddess Syria . . .Sukona, punish, show your power. I register those who had any knowledge of it and those who took part in it. I register him, his head, his soul, the sinews of the one who stole the necklace/bracelet, and of those who know anything about it and who took part in it. I register the genital and the private parts of the one who stole it; and of those who took and stole the necklace , the hands . . . from head to feet. . . toenails . . . of those who took the necklace . . . those who had any knowledge of it . . . whether man or woman."
Size: 14 x 14cm; Material: Lead tablet; Holes/Nails: Neither; Location/ Date Found: Under a house on Delos, Greece; Deities: Sukonaioi, Syria Sukona; Names: None; Reason for Curse: Theft of a necklace. [600]

Translation: "Secundina commands of Mercurius and Moltinus, concerning whoever has stolen two necklaces worth fourteen *denarii*, that deceitful Cacus remove him and his fortune, just as hers were taken, the very things which she hands over to you so that you will track them down. She hands them over to you so that you will track them down and separate him from his fortune, from his family and from his dear ones. She commands you on this, you must bring them to justice."
Size: 5.7 x 2.6cm; Material: Lead; Holes/Nails: Neither; Location/ Date Found: Burial site in Wilten, Austria; Deities: Mercury, Moltinus, Cacus; Names: Secundina; Reason for Curse: Theft two necklaces. [601]

---

[600] Gager, *Curse Tablets and Binding Spells of the Ancient World,* 188. Originally in Greek, translated by Gager.

[601] Gager, *Curse Tablets and Binding Spells of the Ancient World*, 198-199. Translated by Gager.

Bibliography

Adams, J. N. "British Latin: The Text, Interpretation and Language of the Bath Curse Tablets." *Britannia* 23 (1992): 1-26.

-----. "The New Vindolanda Writing-Tablets." *The Classical Quarterly*, New Series 53 no. 2 (2003): 530-575.

Ainsworth, C. J. and H. B. A. Ratcliffe-Densham. "Spectroscopy and a Roman Cremation from Sompting, Sussex." *Britannia* 5 (1974): 310-316.

Aldhouse-Green, Miranda. "Gallo-British Deities and their Shrines." In *A Companion to Roman Britain*. Edited by Malcolm Todd. Malden, MA: Blackwell Publishing, 2004.

Alcock, Joan P. *Daily Life of the Pagan Celts*. Oxford: Greenwood World Publishing, 2009.

-----. *Food in Roman Britain*. Stroud: Tempus, 2001.

-----. "The Concept of Genius in Roman Britain." In *Pagan Gods and Shrines of the Roman Empire*. Edited by Martin Henig and Anthony King. Oxford: Oxford University Committee for Archaeology, 1986.

-----."The People." In *A Companion to Roman Britain*. Edited by Peter A. Clayton. Oxford: Phaidon, 1980.

Allason-Jones, Lindsay. *Daily Life in Roman Britain*. Oxford: Greenwood World Publishing, 2008.

-----. "The Family in Roman Britain." In *A Companion to Roman Britain*. Edited by Malcolm Todd. Malden, MA: Blackwell Publishing, 2004.

Ankarloo, Bengt and Stuart Clark, ed. *Witchcraft and Magic in Europe: Ancient Greece and Rome*. Philadelphia: University of Pennsylvania Press, 1999.

Apuleius Madaurensis. *Apulei Apologia siue Pro Se de Magia Liber*. Commentary by H. E. Butler & A. S. Owen. Oxford: Clarendon Press, 1914.

Assmann, Jan. "When Justice Fails: Jurisdiction and Imprecation in Ancient Egypt and the Near East." *The Journal of Egyptian Archaeology* 78 (1992): 149-162.

Audollent, Augustus. Marie Henri, translator. *Defixionum Tabellae*. Frankfurt: Minerva, 1967.

Balsdon, J. P. V. D. "The Veracity of Caesar." *Greece & Rome*, Second Series, Vol. 4, No. 1 (1957): 19-28.

Barker, Philip. "Excavations on the Site of the Baths Basilica at Wroxeter 1966-1974: An Interim Report." *Britannia* 6 (1975): 106-117.

Bayliss, Andrew J. "Curse-Tablets as Evidence: Identifying the Elusive 'Peiraikoi Soldiers.'" *Zeitschrift für Papyrologie und Epigraphik* 144 (2003): 125-140.

Betz, Hans Dieter, ed. *The Greek Magical Papyri in Translation.* Chicago: University of Chicago Press, 1986.

Birely, Anthony R. *The People of Roman Britain.* Berkeley: University of California Press, 1980.

-----. "The Date of the Temple of Sulis Minerva at Bath." *Britannia* 10 (1979): 101-107.

Boon, George C. *Roman Silchester: The Archaeology of a Romano-British Town.* London: Max Parrish, 1957.

Boulakia, Jean David C. "Lead in the Roman World." *American Journal of Archaeology* 76 no. 2 (1972): 139-144.

Bowman, Alan K. *Life and Letters on the Roman Frontier: Vindolanda and Its People.* New York: Routledge, 1994.

-----. *The Roman Writing Tablets from Vindolanda.* London: British Museum Publications, 1983.

Bowman, Alan K. and J. David Thomas. *Vindolanda: The Latin Writing Tablets.* Gloucester, UK: Alan Sutton Publishing, 1983.

-----. "New Writing-Tablets from Vindolanda." *Britannia* 27 (1996): 299-328.

Brailsford, J. W. "Roman Writing-Tablets from London." *The British Museum Quarterly* 12, no. 2 (1954): 39-40.

Breeze, David J. *Roman Frontiers in Britain.* London: Bristol Classical Press, 2007.

Brichto, Herbert Chanan. *The Problem of 'Curse' in the Hebrew Bible.* Philadelphia: Society of Biblical Literature, 1963.

Broughton, T.R.S. *The Romanization of African Proconsularis.* Baltimore: Johns Hopkins Press, 1929.

Brunaux, Jean Louis. *The Celtic Gauls: Gods, Rites and Sanctuaries.* Translated by Daphne Nash. London: Seaby, 1988.

Burgess, Jeremy. "Formulaic Constructions in Curse Tablets from Roman Britain." MA thesis, University of Hawaii at Manoa, 2002.

Burnham, B. C., L. J. F. Keppie, A. S. Esmonde Bleary, M. W. C. Hassall, and R. S. O. Tomlin. "Roman Britain in 1992." *Britannia* 24 (1993): 267-322.

-----. "Roman Britain in 1993." *Britannia* 25 (1994): 245-314.

-----. "Roman Britain in 1994." *Britannia* 26 (1995): 325-390.

-----. "Roman Britain in 1995." *Britannia* 27 (1996): 389-547.

Burnham, B. C., F. Hunter, A. P. Fitzpatrick, M. W. C. Hassall, and R. S. O. Tomlin. "Roman Britain in 2002." *Britannia* 34 (2003): 293-382.

Burnham, B. C., F. Hunter, A. P. Fitzpatrick, S. Worrell, M. W. C. Hassall, and R. S. O. Tomlin. "Roman Britain in 2003." *Britannia* 35 (2004): 253-349.

-----. "Roman Britain in 2005." *Britannia* 37 (2006): 369-488.

Burl, Aubrey. *Prehistoric Avebury*. 2nd edition. New Haven: Yale University Press, 2002.

Burrell, Barbara. "'Curse Tablets' from Caesarea." *Near Eastern Archeology* Vol. 61 No. 2 (1998): 128.

Butcher, Sarnia A. "Enamels from Roman Britain." In *Ancient Monuments and Their Interpretation: Essays Presented to A. J. Taylor*. Edited by M. R. Apted, R. Gilyard-Beer, and A. D. Saunders. London: Phillimore & Co., 1977.

Caesar, Gaius Julius. *Gallic War Book VI*. Edited by E.S. Shuckburgh. Cambridge: Cambridge University Press, 1950.

Cato. *De Agri Cultura*. Leipzig: Teveneri, 1895.

Chadwick, Nora K. *Celtic Britain*. New York: Frederick A. Praeger, 1964.

Champion, Timothy. "Prehistoric Kent." In *The Archaeology of Kent to AD 800*, edited by John H Williams. Woodbridge, UK: Boydell Press and Kent County Council, 2007.

Chapman, E. M., F. Hunter, P. Booth, P. Wilson, S., Worrell and R. S. O. Tomlin. "Roman Britain in 2008." *Britannia* 40 (2009): 219-363.

Cicero, *De Deivinatione*. Stutgardiae: in aedibus B. G. Teubneri, 1965.

Ciraolo, Leda Jean. "Supernatural Assistants in the Greek Magical Papyri." In *Ancient Magic and Ritual Power*, edited by Marvin Meyer and Paul Mirecki. Boston: Brill Academic Publishers, 2001.

Clarke, Giles. *The Roman Cemetery at Lankhills*. Oxford: Clarendon Press, 1979.

Coles, J. M. and A. F. Harding. *The Bronze Age in Europe*. London: Methuen & Co., 1979.

Collingwood, R.G. *Roman Britain*. Oxford: Clarendon Press, 1966.

-----. *Roman Inscriptions and Sculptures Belonging to the Society of Antiquaries of Newcastle Upon Tyne*. Newcastle-Upon-Tyne: Northumberland Press, 1929.

Collingwood, R. G. and J. N, L. Myres. *Roman Britain and the English Settlements*. Second edition. Oxford: Clarendon Press, 1937.

Collingwood, R.G. and Ian Richmond. *The Archeology of Roman Britain*. London: Methuem & Co., 1930.

Collingwood, R.G. and R. P. Wright, ed. *The Roman Inscriptions of Britain*. 2 Volumes. Gloucester: Alan Sutton Publishing, 1990.

Croom, Alexandra. "Personal Ornament." In *A Companion to Roman Britain*. Edited by Malcolm Todd. Malden, MA: Blackwell Publishing, 2004.

Curbera, Jamie B. and David R. Jordan. "A Curse Tablet from the 'Industrial District' Near the Athenian Agora." *Hesperia* 67 no. 2 (1998): 215-218.

Curbera, Jamie B., Marta Sierra Delage, and Isabel Velázquez. "A Bilingual Curse Tablet from Barchín del Hoyo (Cuenca, Spain)" *Zeitschrift für Papyrologie und Epigraphik* 125 (1999): 279-283.

Cunliffe, Barry. *Danebury: An Iron Age Hillfort in Hampshire.* 2 Volumes. London: Council for British Archaeology, 1984.

-----.*Excavations at Portchester Castle Vol. 2: Saxon.* London: The Society of Antiquaries of London, 1976.

-----. *Rome and the Barbarians.* New York: Henry Z Walck Inc, 1975.

-----. *Roman Bath Discovered.* London: Routledge and Kegan Paul, 1984.

-----. *The City of Bath.* Gloucester: Alan Sutton, 1986.

-----. "The Sanctuary of Sulis Minerva at Bath: A Brief Review." In *Pagan Gods and Shrines of the Roman Empire.* Edited by Martin Henig and Anthony King. Oxford: Oxford University Committee for Archaeology, 1986.

-----. *Wessex to AD 1000.* London: Longman, 1993.

D'Ambra, Eve. "Racing with Death: Circus Sarcophagi and the Commemoration of Children in Roman Italy." *Hesperia Supplements* 41 (2007): 339-351

de la Bèdoyère, Guy. *Roman Britain: A New History.* New York: Thames & Hudson, 2006.

Dickie, Matthew W. *Magic and Magicians in the Greco-Roman World.* London: Routledge, 2003.

Dio, Cassius. *Roman History.* Translated by Earnest Cary. Cambridge, MA: Harvard University Press, 1982.

Diodorus of Sicily. *The Library of History*, Vol. 3. Translated by C. H. Oldfather. Cambridge, MA: Harvard University Press, 1939.

Drury, P. J. "Non-Classical Religious Buildings in Iron Age and Roman Britain: A Review." In *Temples, Churches and Religion: Recent Research in Roman Britain.* Edited by Warwick Rodwell. Oxford: British Archeological Reports, 1980.

Dyer, James. *Southern England: An Archeological Guide, the Prehistoric and Roman Remains.* Park Ridge, N.J.: Noyes Press, 1973.

Evans, Ulick R. *An Introduction to Metallic Corrosion.* New York: St. Martin's Press, 1963.

Faraone, Christopher A. *Ancient Greek Love Magic.* Cambridge, Mass: Harvard University Press, 1999.

Faulkner, Neil. *The Decline and Fall of Roman Britain.* Stroud, UK: Tempus Publishing, 2004.

Ferguson, John. *The Religions of the Roman Empire.* Ithaca, NY: Cornell University Press, 1970.

Fraser, A. D. "The Ancient Curse: Some Analogies." *The Classical Journal* 17, no. 8 (1922): 454-460.

Frere, S. S., M W. C. Hassall, and R. S. O. Tomlin. "Roman Britain in 1982." *Britannia* 14 (1983): 280-356.

-----. "Roman Britain in 1983." *Britannia* 15 (1984): 266-356.

-----. "Roman Britain in 1985." *Britannia* 17 (1986): 363-454.

-----. "Roman Britain in 1986." *Britannia* 18 (1987): 301-377.

-----. "Roman Britain in 1987." *Britannia* 19 (1988): 415-508.

-----. "Roman Britain in 1988." *Britannia* 20 (1989): 258-345.

Frere, S. S. and R. S. O. Tomlin. "Roman Britain in 1990." *Britannia* 22 (1991): 222-311.

Fulford, Michael. "Economic Structures." In *A Companion to Roman Britain*. Edited by Malcolm Todd. Malden, MA: Blackwell Publishing, 2004.

Gager, John G, ed. *Curse Tablets and Binding Spells from the Ancient World.* New York: Oxford University Press, 1992.

Galliou, Patrick. "Three East Gaulish Brooches Found in Britain." *Britannia* 12 (1981): 288-290.

Goodburn, R., M W. C. Hassall, R. S. O. Tomlin. "Roman Britain in 1978." *Britannia* 10 (1979): 268-356.

Graf, Fritz. "Excluding the Charming: The Development of the Greek Concept of Magic." In *Ancient Magic and Ritual Power*, edited by Marvin Meyer and Paul Mirecki. Boston: Brill Academic Publishers, 2001.

-----. *Magic in the Ancient World.* Translated by Franklin Philip. Cambridge, Mass.: Harvard University Press, 1997

-----. "Theories of Magic in Antiquity." In *Magic and Ritual in the Ancient World*, edited by Paul Mirecki and Marvin Meyer. Leiden: Brill, 2002.

Green, H. J. M. "Religious Cults at Roman Godmanchester." In *Pagan Gods and Shrines of the Roman Empire*. Edited by Martin Henig and Anthony King. Oxford: Oxford University Committee for Archaeology, 1986.

Green, Miranda J. "Jupiter, Taranis and the Solar Wheel." In *Pagan Gods and Shrines of the Roman Empire*. Edited by Martin Henig and Anthony King. Oxford: Oxford University Committee for Archaeology, 1986.

-----. *The Gods of Roman Britain*. Aylesbury, UK: Shire Publications, 1983.

-----. *The Religions of Civilian Roman Britain*. Oxford: British Archaeological Reports, 1976.

Greene, J. Patrick. "Bath and Other Small Western Towns." In *The 'Small Towns' of Roman Britain: Papers Presented to Conference, Oxford 1975*. Edited by Warwick Rodwell and Trevor Rowley. Oxford: British Archaeological Reports, 1975.

Grew, F. O., M. W. C. Hassall, and R. S. O. Tomlin. "Roman Britain in 1980." *Britannia* 12 (1981): 314-396.

Guide to the Antiquities of Roman Britain. London: The Trustees of the British Museum, 1964.

Hamp, Eric P. "Social Gradience in British Spoken Latin." *Britannia* 6 (1975): 150-162.

Harris, William V. *Ancient Literacy*. Cambridge, M.A.: Harvard University Press, 1989.

Haselgrove, Colin. "Society and Polity in Late Iron Age Britain." In *A Companion to Roman Britain*. Edited by Malcolm Todd. Malden, MA: Blackwell Publishing, 2004.

Hassall, M. W. C. "Altars, Curses and Other Epigraphic Evidence." In *Temples, Churches and Religion: Recent Research in Roman Britain*. Edited by Warwick Rodwell. Oxford: British Archeological Reports, 1980.

Hassall, M. W. C., D. R. Wilson, R. P. Wright, and J. Rea. "Roman Britain in 1971." *Britannia* 3 (1972): 299-367.

Haverfield, F. *Catalogue of the Roman Inscribed and Sculptured Stones in the Grosvenor Museum, Chester*. Chester: Chester and North Wales Archaeological Society, 1900.

-----. *The Romanization of Britain*. 4th edition. Westport, Conn: Greenwood Press, 1979.

Haverfield, F. and H. Stuart Jones. "Some Representative Examples of Romano-British Sculpture." *The Journal of Roman Studies* 2 (1912): 121-152.

Henig, Martin. "Roman Religion and Roman Culture." In *A Companion to Roman Britain*. Edited by Malcolm Todd. Malden, MA: Blackwell Publishing, 2004.

-----. *The Art of Roman Britain*. Ann Arbor: The University of Michigan Press, 1995.

-----. *The Heirs of King Verica: Culture and Politics in Roman Britain*. Stroud, UK: Tempus Publishing, 2002.

Hind, John. "Whose Head on the Bath Temple-Pediment?" *Britannia* 27 (1996): 358-360.

Hingley, Richard. *The Recovery of Roman Britain 1586-1906: A Colony so Fertile*. Oxford: Oxford University Press, 2008.

Hollmann, Alexander. "A Curse Tablet from the Circus at Antioch." *Zeitschrift für Papyrologie und Epigraphik* 145 (2003): 67-82.

Hope, Valerie M. "Word and Pictures: The Interpretation of Romano-British Tombstones." *Britannia* Vol. 28 (1997): 245-258.

Horsley, John. *Britannia Romana or the Roman Antiquities of Britain*. Newcastle-upon-Tyne: Frank Graham, 1974.

Hutchinson, Valerie J. *Bacchus in Roman Britain: The Evidence for His Cult*, Vol. 1. Oxford: B.A.R., 1986.

Jentoft-Nilsen, Marit. "A Lead Curse Tablet" *The J. Paul Getty Museum Journal* 8 (1980): 199-201.

Johns, Catherine. "A Roman Bronze Statuette of Epona." *British Museum Quarterly* 36, no. 1/2 (1971): 37-41.

-----. *The Jewellery of Roman Britain: Celtic and Classical Traditions.* Ann Arbor: University of Michigan Press, 1996.

Jones, Michael E. *The End of Roman Britain.* Ithaca: Cornell University Press, 1996.

Jordan, David. "A Curse on Charioteers and Horses at Rome." *Zeitschrift für Papyrologie und Epigraphik* 141 (2002): 141-147.

-----. "A Curse Tablet from a Well in the Athenian Agora." *Zeitschrift für Papyrologie und Epigraphick* 19 (1975): 245-248.

-----. "Defixiones from a Well Near the Southwest Corner of the Athenian Agora." *Hesperia* 54 no. 3 (1985): 205-255.

-----. "Inscribed Lead Tablets from the Games in the Sanctuary of Poseidon." *Hesperia* 63 no. 1 (1994): 111-126.

-----. "'Remedium Amoris,' a Curse from Cumae." *Mnemosyne*, 4th series, Vol. 56, Fasc. 6 (2003): 666-679.

Keay, Simon. "Innovation and Adaptation: The Contribution of Rome to Urbanism in Iberia." In *Social Complexity and the Development of Towns in Iberia: From the Copper Age to the Second Century AD.* Edited by Barry Cunliffe and Simon Keay. Oxford: Oxford University Press, 1995.

Keppie, L. J. F, A. S. Esmonde Cleary, M. W. C. Hassall, R. S. O. Tomlin, and Barry C. Burnham. "Roman Britain in 1997." *Britannia* 29 (1998): 365-445.

-----. "Roman Britain in 1998." *Britannia* 30 (1999): 319-386.

King, Anthony. "Animal Remains from Temples in Roman Britain."*Britannia* 36 (2005): 329-369.

Legg, Rodney. *Romans in Britain.* London: Heinemann, 1983.

Lewis, M. J. T. *Temples in Roman Britain.* Cambridge: Cambridge University Press, 1966.

Ling, Roger. "The Seasons in Romano-British Mosaic Pavements." *Britannia* 14 (1983): 13-22.

Little, Lester K. *Benedictine Maledictions: Liturgical Cursing in Romanesque France.* Ithaca, NY: Cornell University Press, 1993.

Liversidge, Joan. *Furniture in Roman Britain.* London: Alec Tiranti Ltd., 1955.

Lowe, J. E. *Magic and Latin Literature.* Oxford: Basil Blackwell, 1929.

Lucan. *Pharsalia.* Edited by C. E. Haskins. Hildesheim: G. Olms, 1971.

Luck, Georg, ed. *Arcana Mundi: Magic and the Occult in the Greek and Roman Worlds,* 2nd ed. Baltimore: John Hopkins University Press, 2006.

MacDonald, J. L. "Religion." In *The Roman Cemetery at Lankhills.* Edited by Giles Clarke. Oxford: Clarendon Press, 1979.

Mann, J. C. "Spoken Latin in Britain as Evidenced in the Inscriptions." *Britannia* 2 (1971): 218-224.

Martinez, David. "'May She Neither Eat Nor Drink': Love Magic and Vows of Abstinence." In *Ancient Magic and Ritual Power*, edited by Marvin Meyer and Paul Mirecki. Boston: Brill Academic Publishers, 2001.

Mattingly, David J. and R. Bruce Hitchner. "Roman Africa: An Archaeological Review." *The Journal of Roman Studies* Vol. 85 (1995): 165-213.

McWhirr, Alan, Linda Viner, and Calvin Wells. *Romano-British Cemeteries at Cirencester*. Cirencester: Cirencester Excavation Committee, 1982.

Mercer, Samuel A. B. "The Malediction in Cuneiform Inscriptions." *Journal of the American Oriental Society* 34 (1915): 282-309.

Merrifeld, Ralph. *Roman London*. London: Cassell, 1969.

-----."The London Hunter-God." In *Pagan Gods and Shrines of the Roman Empire*. Edited by Martin Henig and Anthony King. Oxford: Oxford University Committee for Archaeology, 1986.

Mierse, William E. *Temples and Towns in Roman Iberia: The Social and Architectural Dynamics of Sanctuary Design from the Third Century B. C. to the Third Century A. D.* Berkeley: University of California Press, 1999.

Millett, Martin. "Art in the 'Small Towns': 'Celtic' or 'Classical'?" In *Roman Life and Art in Britain: A Celebration in Honor of the Eighteenth Birthday of Jocelyn Toynbee*. Vol. 2. Edited by Julian Munby and Martin Henig. Oxford: British Archaeological Reports, 1977.

Muckelroy, K. W. "Enclosed Ambulatories in Romano-Celtic Temples in Britain." *Britannia* 7 (1976): 173-191.

Mullen, Alex. "Linguistic Evidence for 'Romanization': Continuity and Change in Romano-British Onomastics; A Study of the Epigraphic Record with Particular Reference to Bath." *Britannia* 38 (2007): 35-61.

Nash-Williams, V.E. and A. H. *Catalogue of the Roman Inscribed and Sculpted Stones Found at Caerleon, Monmouthshire*. Cardiff: National Museum of Wales and Press Board of the University of Wales, 1935.

Nelson, A. "Abracadabra." *Eranos* 44 (1946): 326-336.

Niblett, Rosalind. "The Native Elite and their Funerary Practices from the First Century BC to Nero." In *A Companion to Roman Britain*. Edited by Malcolm Todd. Malden, MA: Blackwell Publishing, 2004.

Ogden, Daniel. *Greek and Roman Necromancy*. Princeton: Princeton University Press, 2001.

-----. *Magic, Witchcraft, and Ghosts in the Greek and Roman Worlds: A Sourcebook*, 2nd ed. Oxford: Oxford University Press, 2009.

-----. *Night's Black Agents: Witches, Wizards, and the Dead in the Ancient World.* London and New York: Hambledon Continuum, 2008.

Onians, Richard Broxton. *The Origins of European Thought: About the Body, the Mind, the Soul, the World, Time and Fate.* Cambridge: Cambridge University Press, 1951.

Parrish, David. "Two Mosaics from Roman Tunisia: An African Variation of the Season Theme." *American Journal of Archaeology* 83 no. 3 (1979): 279-285.

Pearson, F. R. *Roman Yorkshire.* East Ardsley, UK: EP Publishing, 1973.

Pearson, Michael Parker. *English Heritage Book of Bronze Age Britain.* London: B. T. Batsford, 1993.

Petts, David. "Landscape and Cultural Identity in Roman Britain." In *Cultural Identity in the Roman Empire*, edited by Ray Laurence and Joanne Berry. London and New York: Routledge, 1998.

Philp, B. J., Ralph Merrifield, Geoffrey Dannell, Peter Couldrey, M. Y. Stant, and Wendy Williams. "The Forum of Roman London: Excavations of 1968-9." *Britannia* 8 (1977): 1-64.

Plato. *Laws* Vol. II. Translated by R. G. Bury. Cambridge, MA: Harvard University Press, 1984.

Pliny the Elder. *Natural History.* Vol. IV. Edited by H. Rackham. London: William Heinmann Ltd., 1968.

-----. *Natural History.* Vol. VIII. Edited by W. H. S. Jones. London: William Heinemann Ltd., 1963.

Pollard, Elizabeth Ann. "Witch-Crafting in Roman Literature and Art: New Thoughts on an Old Image." *Magic Ritual, and Witchcraft* 3, no.2 (2009): 119-155.

Powell, Kelly. "The Nails" In Life and Death in a *Roman City: Excavation of a Roman Cemetery with a Mass Grave at 120-122 London Road, Gloucester*, edited by Andrew Simmonds, Nicholas Marquez-Grant and Louis Loe. Oxford: Oxford Archeological Monograph No. 6, 2008.

Rankov, N. B., M. W. C. Hassall, and R. S. O. Tomlin. "Roman Britain in 1981." *Britannia* 13 (1981): 328-422.

Raybould, Marilynne E. *A Study of Inscribed Material from Roman Britain: An Inquiry into Some Aspects of Literacy in Romano-British Society.* Oxford: Archaeopress, 1999.

Revell, Louise. *Roman Imperialism and Local Identities.* Cambridge: Cambridge University Press, 2009.

Richmond, I. A. and J. M. C. Toynbee. "The Temple of Sulis-Minerva at Bath." *The Journal of Roman Studies* 45 (1955): 97-105.

Rives, James B. "Magic in Roman Law: The Reconstruction of a Crime." *Classical Antiquity* 22, no. 2 (2003): 313-339.

Rivet, A. L. F. "Summing Up: The Classification of Minor Towns and Related Settlements." In *The 'Small Towns' of Roman Britain: Papers Presented to Conference, Oxford 1975*. Edited by Warwick Rodwell and Trevor Rowley. Oxford: British Archaeological Reports, 1975.

Rodwell, Warwick, ed. *Temples, Churches and Religion: Recent Research in Roman Britain with a Gazetteer of Romano-Celtic Temples in Continental Europe*. Oxford: BAR British Series 775, 1980.

Ross, Anne. *Pagan Celtic Britain: Studies in Iconography and Tradition*. London: Routledge and Kegan Paul, 1967.

Rossi, Andreola. "The Camp of Pompey: Strategy of Representation in Caesar's *Bellum Ciuile*." *The Classical Journal*. Vol 95, No. 3 (2000): 239-256.

Seebohm, Frederic. *The Tribal System in Wales*. London: Longmans, Green & Co., 1895.

Sellwood, Lyn. "The Celtic Coins." In *The Temple of Sulis Minerva at Bath*. Vol. 2, *The Finds from the Sacred Spring*. Edited by Barry Cunnliffe. Oxford: Oxford University Committee for Archeology, 1988.

Shottler, David. *Roman Britain*. 2nd edition. London: Routledge, 2004.

Smith, Leslie F. "A Pagan Parallel to 'Curse of Ernulphus.'" *The Classical Journal* 46, no. 6 (1951): 303-304.

Solinus, Caius Julius. *Collectanea Rerum Memorabilium*. Society for the Promotion of Roman Studies. "Roman Britain in 1957: I. Sites Explored: II. Inscriptions." *The Journal of Roman Studies* 48, no.1/2 (1958): 130-155.

Stead, Ian M. *Excavations at Winterton Roman Villa and other Roman Sites in North Lincolnshire*. London: Her Majesty's Stationary Office, 1976.

Stewart, P. C. N. "Inventing Britain: The Roman Creation and Adaptation of an Image." *Britannia* 26 (1995): 1-10.

Strabo. *The Geography of Strabo*. Vol. 1. Translated by H, C, Hamilton. London: G. Bell and Sons, 1912.

Stratton, Kimberly B. *Naming the Witch: Magic, Ideology, and Stereotype in the Ancient World*. New York: Columbia University Press, 2007.

Tacitus, Cornelius. *The Life of Cnœus Julius Agricola*. Translated by Alfred John Church and William Jackson Brodribb. New York: Random House, 1942.

-----. *The Annals*. Volume 5. Translated by John Jackson. Cambridge, MA: Harvard University Press, 1981.

Tavenner, Eugene. *Studies in Magic from Latin Literature*. New York, AMS Press, 1966.

Tomlin, R.S.O. "A Bilingual Roman Charm for Health and Victory." *Zeitschrift für Papyrologie und Epigraphick* 149 (2004): 259-266.

-----."Roman Manuscripts from Carlisle: The Ink-Written Tablets." *Britannia* 29 (1998): 31-84.

-----. "The Curse Tablets." In *The Temple of Sulis Minerva at Bath*. Vol. 2, *The Finds from the Sacred Spring*. Edited by Barry Cunliffe. Oxford: Oxford University Committee for Archeology, 1988.

Townend, G. B. "Some Rhetorical Battle-Pictures in Dio." *Hermes* Vol. 92, No. 4 (1964): 467-481.

Turner, Eric G. "A Curse from Nottinghamshire." *The Journal of Roman Studies* 53 no. 1/2 (1963): 122-124.

Turner, Eric G. and Otto Skutsch. "A Roman Writing-Tablet from London." *The Journal of Roman Studies* 50 (1960): 108-111.

Turner, Victor W. *The Ritual Process: Structure and Anti-Structure.* Chicago: Aldine Publishing Company, 1969.

Varro, Marcus Terentius. Roland Kent, translator. *On the Latin Language.* Vol. I. Cambridge, Mass.: Harvard university press, 1938.

Versnel, H.S. "The Poetics of the Magical Charm: An Essay in the Power of Words." In *Magic and Ritual in the Ancient World*, edited by Paul Mirecki and Marvin Meyer. Leiden: Brill, 2002.

Wacher, John. *A Portrait of Roman Britain.* London: Routledge, 2000.

-----. *Roman Britain.* London: J.M. Dent & Sons, 1980.

Walters, H. B. *Catalogue of the Silver Plate (Greek, Etruscan and Roman) in the British Museum.* London: Trustees of the British Museum, 1921.

Ward-Perkins, Bryan. *The Fall of Rome and the End of Civilization.* Oxford: Oxford University Press, 2005.

Watts, Dorothy. *Religion in Late Roman Britain: Forces of Change.* London: Routledge, 1998.

Webster, Graham. *Celtic Religion in Roman Britain.* Totown, NJ: Barnes & Noble Books, 1986.

-----. *The British Celts and Their Gods Under Rome.* London: B. T. Batsford Ltd., 1986.

-----. *The Roman Invasion of Britain.* London: Routledge, 1980.

-----. "What the Britons Required from the Gods as Seen Through the Pairing of Roman and Celtic Deities and the Character of Votive Offerings." In *Pagan Gods and Shrines of the Roman Empire*. Edited by Martin Henig and Anthony King. Oxford: Oxford University Committee for Archaeology, 1986.

Wenham, Leslie P. *The Romano-British Cemetery at Trentholme Drive, York.* London: Her Majesty's Stationary Office, 1968.

Wild, John Peter. "Textiles and Dress." In *A Companion to Roman Britain*. Edited by Malcolm Todd. Malden, MA: Blackwell Publishing, 2004.

-----. *Textile Manufacture in the Northern Roman Provinces*. Cambridge: Cambridge University Press, 1970.

Wilson, D. R. and R. P. Wright. "Roman Britain in 1968: I. Sites Explored: II. Inscriptions." *The Journal of Roman Studies* 59 no.1/2 (1969): 198-246.

Wilson, D. R., R. P. Wright, and M. W. C. Hassall. "Roman Britain in 1970." *Britannia* 2 (1971): 243-304.

-----. "Roman Britain in 1972." *Britannia* 4 (1973): 271-337.

Woodward, Roger D. *Indo-European Sacred Space: Vedic and Roman Cult*. Urbana and Chicago: University of Illinois Press, 2006.

Woolf, Greg. *Becoming Roman: The Origins of Provincial Civilization in Gaul*. Cambridge: Cambridge University Press, 1998.

-----. "Beyond Romans and Native." *World Archaeology* 28 no. 3 (1997): 339-350.

Wright, Thomas. *Uriconium: A Historical Account of the Ancient Roman City and of the Excavations Made Upon its Site at Wroxeter in Shropshire*. London: Longmans, Green, & Co., 1872.

INDEX

Made in the USA
Middletown, DE
11 August 2024

58916345R00084